101
Amazing
Achievements

101
Amazing
Achievements

Bev Spencer

Illustrations by
Bill Dickson

Scholastic Canada Ltd.

Toronto New York London Auckland Sydney
Mexico City New Delhi Hong Kong Buenos Aires

Scholastic Canada Ltd.
175 Hillmount Road, Markham, Ontario L6C 1Z7, Canada

Scholastic Inc.
555 Broadway, New York, NY 10012, USA

Scholastic Australia Pty Limited
PO Box 579, Gosford, NSW 2250, Australia

Scholastic New Zealand Limited
Private Bag 94407, Greenmount, Auckland, New Zealand

Scholastic Ltd.
Villiers House, Clarendon Avenue, Leamington Spa,
Warwickshire CV32 5PR, UK

National Library of Canada Cataloguing in Publication

Spencer, Beverley
Made in Canada : 101 amazing achievements
Includes index.
ISBN 0-439-98852-7
1. Canada—Miscellanea—Juvenile literature. I. Title.
FC58.S69 2002   j971   C2002-900334-2
F1008.2.S69 2002

6 5 4 3 2 1   Printed in Canada   03 04 05 06 07

Table of Contents

To Lisa, a very, very special friend

Introduction

Why should you read this book? Because there are so many AMAZING, FUNNY and FASCINATING things that have been made in Canada, dreamed up in Canada, and invented by Canadians. And you probably don't know about most of them!! Canada is brimming over with inventors and innovators. Canadians have wacky ideas and brilliant ideas. Canadians make startling discoveries and life-saving devices. Canadians do astonishing things, heroic things, things that will make you feel proud. Canadians dare to dream, and find ways to make their dreams come true. But for some strange reason, Canadians don't know nearly enough about their inventors, heroes, innovators and scientists. So open up this book, and be prepared to be surprised. I was.

Of course, by the time you read this book, even *more* creative Canadian inventions will have been made.

And remember, if you think that someone else actually was the first to do or make something you read about in *Made in Canada*, stay calm. The truth is that sometimes people invent or discover the *same* thing completely independently, in different places. Scientists say that this is because, as technology advances, there's a kind of readiness for a new invention. Enough groundwork has been laid by those who came before for a clever mind to make another leap forward. It happens.

3-D Jigsaw Puzzles Revolutionize a 200-Year-Old Game

Sometimes an innovation changes a game so much that a whole new group of players discovers it. That's what happened in 1990 when Paul Gallant of Montreal came up with a three-dimensional jigsaw puzzle at his kitchen table. He had been trying for years to find a new wrinkle on the old game. Excited, he went to his garage and made the first 3-D puzzle — The Old Mansion. It stood up like a model of a house. A whole new form of entertainment was born that day, when Gallant used foam backing to make the cardboard puzzle pieces stick together securely enough to stand up.

Gallant thought he was on to something, but would it catch on? He sent The Old Mansion to F.A.O. Schwartz, the American toy store. The response was fast and overwhelming. Gallant had to rush fifteen workers into his garage to fill a big order. His company, Wrebbit, was off to a flying start, and hasn't touched down yet. In 1999 Wrebbit's sales passed 30 million Puzz-3D puzzles. Over 85 percent of the puzzles are shipped to customers outside of Canada, with more than 60 countries showering Wrebbit with awards, including Most Innovative Toy and an Excellence Award for Canadian exports. Gallant has reached an audience that never touched a jigsaw puzzle before, too. Only ten years ago jigsaw puzzles were mainly bought and assembled by women or children, but about half of Wrebbit's sales go to men. Why the change? Gallant says putting his puzzles together is a bit like constructing buildings.

DAD, CAN *I* PLAY WITH MY 3-D PUZZLE NOW?

A lot of Wrebbit's success is due to some brilliant marketing moves. Gallant got licences to make Cinderella's Castle, Snow White and The Lion King puzzles in 3-D from Disney. He has agreements to make Star Wars and Sesame Street puzzles. And he attracts attention at international toy fairs by making enormous, showy 3-D puzzles. In 1997 he made a panoramic train set filled with fascinating details, 10 metres long, with mini cameras transmitting a scenic route. The train display visited eight European and American cities. In 1998 a team built a reproduction of the *Titanic* that was 13 metres long, 3.6 metres wide and 1.5 metres high, made out of 30,000 puzzle pieces. In 1999 Wrebbit re-created a car from the famous 1920s Orient Express Train, at 75 percent of life size. The luxurious details of the inside of the car, including passengers, chairs and tables, as well as the outside, were all made of Puzz-3D puzzle pieces. Even at the biggest international toy fairs, these are showstoppers. Wrebbit fans have also made a life-sized Grand Prix racing car.

The more wonderful puzzles the company makes, the more it sells. Puzzle fans can get replica castles, cathedrals and towers, like England's Big Ben clock tower and Rome's Saint Peter's Basilica. There are fantasy puzzles too, like The Enchanted Carousel and The Medieval Clock. If that's not enough, players can get the Puzz-3D

CD and assemble Notre Dame de Paris Cathedral on the computer. Once they're done, they can "visit" the cathedral through the CD, too.

Wrebbit's creativity never seems to end. Their latest products are Perfalock Puzzle scenes, the first-ever pliable jigsaw puzzles. Laminated on high-density foam, they are so tough they can be picked up and moved around easily. A howling wolf pack, fall flowers and an ice hockey team are among the new "no-tech" family fun puzzles.

Canadian Game Banishes Boredom

Chris Haney and Scott Abbott could never have imagined what lay in store when they invented a board game based on trivia — fascinating little facts. They called it Trivial Pursuit, but the reaction to the game was anything *but* trivial. Haney's and Abbott's creation went on to become the most commercially successful board game since Monopoly and Scrabble. Families all over the world play it now.

The first version of the game contained six categories of questions — Geography, Entertainment, History, Art and Literature, Science and Nature, and Sports and Leisure. Each of the 1,000 cards in the box contained six questions, with answers on the back. The roll of a die moved each player's token on the board. Answer the trivia question from a particular category correctly, and a player could move toward the finish line.

When they initially created the game, Haney and Abbott had to scramble to produce the first 1,200 test-market copies in the fall of 1981. Success did not come at once . . . but by March of 1982 their assembly line couldn't make enough games to fill the orders flooding in. Sales of Trivial Pursuit topped $2 billion worldwide within a few years, and more than a hundred separate editions of the game now exist, in more than thirty countries.

Play On – Other Games Made in Canada

That's a What?

You don't have to be an artist to be good at Pictionary, but you do need imagination. And your drawings have to make *some* sense. If an apple looks the same as a house when you draw it, the other players on your team won't be able to figure out what word or phrase you want them to guess . . . and you have only sixty seconds to draw the picture! Ready to dust off your drawing pencil and take on your friends?

Rob Angel of Vancouver, British Columbia, invented Pictionary in 1986. A simple idea? Wish you had thought of it? Angel's invention has sold over 15 million copies around the world. Like many inventions, it looks easy only *after* it has been created.

And I Thought You Had Morals!

You think you know your friends? Try playing this game with them. You might get some surprises! What decision would your friends make when what's right and what's wrong aren't very clear? Would they answer the same as you would? Think again.

A Question of Scruples is an ingenious game invented by Henry Makow, a former writer and university professor. In 1985 his game hit the market with a bang, and in 1986 it even outsold Trivial Pursuit. In fact, over 7 million copies have been sold throughout the world.

What makes A Question of Scruples so popular? Players have to decide what they would do in a tricky situation — one that challenges their ethics. Other players then have to try to predict their choices.

Shall We Play on Your Yacht?

The rattle of dice; the throw; a quick count; victory! It's a fast, fun game, and it was made in Canada.

A well-to-do Canadian couple created The Yacht Game in the late 1800s. It's a compact game, easy to play in a small space. Players throw dice from a cup, and try to score highest in categories based on poker. At first it was played at yacht clubs to see who would pay for the drinks, but the inventors wanted copies to give to their friends who enjoyed the game so much. In the 1920s they sold the rights to Edwin S. Lowe, in exchange for a few copies. Lowe changed the name to Yahtzee. Despite the lack of yachts in most people's lives, the game has sold over 40 million copies.

You're Bluffing!

Can you tell when someone is telling a whopper? Do you like a good belly laugh? Yes? Then the game Balderdash is for you. Players make up the meanings of wacky but real words. Only one person has it right, and everyone else is bluffing. But *who* is telling the bizarre truth? If you can zero in on him or her, you'll win the game. It's all for fun, and the real definitions are just as funny as the most ridiculous meanings the players can invent.

Torontonians Paul Toyne and Laura Robinson combined their writing talents and slapstick humour to invent Balderdash. Toyne was an ad writer and Robinson an actor. The Canada Games Company of Downsview, Ontario, has sold over 2.5 million copies worldwide since 1984. That's about $40 million in sales. In Sweden, Balderdash was named Game of the Year. In both Canada and Sweden it was the best-selling game two years in a row. Ten countries have jumped on the Balderdash bandwagon, and the new version, Absolute Balderdash, has five categories to increase the hilarity — words, people, initials, movies and laws.

How did the inventors come up with the game's "stranger than fiction" words? Toyne and Robinson spent eight months of 1984 in the Robarts Library at the University of Toronto, poring over 200 dictionaries. They looked at over 2 million unusual and comical-sounding words. Whew! Then they picked the 2,500 words for the original version of the game. Chances are that players won't know any of them. That makes the game fair. But each word appears in at least one real, bona fide dictionary.

Toyne had wanted to invent a successful game for years, but his biggest thrill is knowing millions of people are enjoying the product of his and Robinson's imaginations.

Malversation: truly terrible words

Porbeagle: a really, really sad dog

Superman Is Half Canadian

Superman, superhero of movies and television shows, has Canadian roots. He started in comic books, drawn by a Canadian artist. He may have morphed into new identities, but he was born in a Canadian mind.

Toronto-born Joe Shuster drew cartoons for the *Toronto Star* and published science fiction magazines on the side. His partner in publishing was American writer Jerome Siegel. The two had met when Shuster studied at the Cleveland School of Art. When they got interested in comic books, they dreamed up Superman and his alter-ego, the mild-mannered Clark Kent. Shuster drew the Man of Steel, and Siegel wrote Superman's dialogue. Shuster based Kent's *Daily Star* and its characters on the *Toronto Star*. Eventually the name of the fictional newspaper was changed to the *Daily Planet*.

Shuster and Siegel had just begun publishing comic books in 1936. When Action Comics offered them $130 for Superman in 1938 it must have seemed like a good deal. They took the money and joined the staff at Action Comics to continue creating their Superman character.

By 1947 Superman had captured the public imagination. No other comic book hero had ever been so famous. The money poured in . . . but to Action Comics, *not* into Shuster's and Siegel's pockets. They were still on salaries, and they wanted more — after all, they had created Superman. The problem was, Action Comics *owned* the character. Shuster and Siegel sued for a percentage of the royalties Superman was earning, but that just got them both fired. Superman lived on, but his creators were getting no profits, and now no credit either.

Shuster stopped drawing. He watched his cousin Frank Shuster, the Canadian comedian, become famous and successful, but he never drew Superman again, and in later life he lost his sight.

Superman became a television series, and later a string of hit movies. In the mid-1970s the first *Superman* movie starring Christopher Reeve earned over $80 million. Siegel had had enough, and sued again. By then the Superman property was owned by DC Comics, and they were ready to make a deal. Future Superman productions would bear the names of its creators, and DC Comics would pay Shuster and Siegel $20,000 a year for life.

Shuster died in Los Angeles, California, in 1992, but his fictional superhero lives on.

And Superman's Canadian roots keep showing. Glenn Ford, who was born in Quebec, played the human father who adopted the Man of Steel in the first *Superman* movie. Margot Kidder, who played Clark Kent's girlfriend, was born in Yellowknife, in the Northwest Territories.

First Documentary Film in the World

American Robert Flaherty came north in 1922 to make the first documentary film in the world. His subject was Canadian, and he made the film in Canada. Never before had a film been called a "documentary," a new word for a film about a real person or event. *Nanook of the North* told the story of an Inuit hunter, and was intended to help people understand life in the Far North. Nanook (literally "the bear") lived in the eastern Arctic, and died two years after the film was released.

This Canadian story set a new standard and format for films. Now documentaries are important to both the television and film industries. Viewers have seen so many of them — films about sharks, shipwrecks and other true stories — that they don't even think about how this type of film was first invented. Without the documentary, TV would be much less interesting.

Do you hate sitting through commercials on TV? What about a commercial as *long* as a film? A Canadian film was the first film ad in the world — an infomercial to promote the prairies. Manitoba farmer James Freer made the film in 1897. It showed life on the Canadian prairies, and was used to encourage people in the United Kingdom to immigrate and settle there.

IMAX – a Canadian Experience

The land rushes toward you, and tilts. The speeding image is so big it seems to surround you; so sharp you feel you could put out a hand and touch it. You feel like you are hurtling through the air, a fly on the windshield of a jet — or maybe even the pilot. Or you are watching the launch of the NASA Space Shuttle, its powerful engine sending out plumes of flame that seem close enough to sear your face! The scene changes. Now you are far beneath the ocean, walking the drowned halls of the *Titanic*, lost in an eerie gloom. Nothing has prepared you for these sensations of speed, power and discovery.

If the movie is this vivid, this overwhelming, it's probably IMAX. The technology that dazzles viewers is Canadian-made. The name IMAX comes from *I* for image and *MAX* for maximum visual impact — the most the eye can see. How big are IMAX films? As high as a six-storey building!

The first permanent IMAX theatre, called Cinesphere, opened at Ontario Place in 1970. The inspiration for IMAX was the "Labyrinth" show created for the 1967 World Exposition in Montreal, co-directed by Colin Low of Alberta, a member of the National Film Board. In this show, multiple screens and projectors were used, giving ten times the information a viewer usually gets from a film.

The most technically advanced film projector in the world was developed in the 1960s. Engineer William Shaw and filmmakers Graeme Ferguson, Robert Kerr and Roman Kroitor, all of Toronto, Ontario, worked on the project. Six million people saw the debut of their system at the Fuji Group Pavilion at Japan's Expo '70. How did the inventors do it? They used 70-millimetre film — the largest film frame in history — to produce crisp, brilliant, giant images. A special side-to-side projector called the "rolling loop" projector had to be created to handle it. Invented by Australian Ron Jones, the projector was adapted by the IMAX inventors to help solve technical challenges posed by projecting film so large.

Audiences were captivated by IMAX's visually stunning shows. In 1990 a fish-eye lens was put on the camera and projector, so the film could be projected onto an enormous domed screen, 24 metres wide. This created the OMNIMAX system, which surrounds you in the film experience, so you seem to be part of the action. Surround sound completes the effect. There are more than 125 permanent IMAX or OMNIMAX theatres around the world.

The screens are made of stretched vinyl, and weigh 360 kilograms. (The film itself can weigh in at a hefty 90 kilograms.) Each frame of IMAX film is now 70 millimetres by 70 millimetres, much larger than 35-millimetre film. A forty-five minute feature uses a whopping 5 kilometres of film.

IMAX screens can show a whale life-sized — 20 metres high by 27 metres wide. Getting these huge images on film is not easy. A large camera, weighing 39 kilograms with lens and film, must be used to take the pictures. But many of the subjects have been worth all that trouble — like the Space Shuttle footage, undersea images of the *Titanic*, and spectacular images of wilderness, coral reefs, mountains and canyons. Viewers can recline in comfort as sound and image carry them where most of us will never go.

IMAX is a long way from the first "deluxe" motion-picture theatre in the world. Why deluxe? It had upholstered seats rather than just ordinary hard chairs. Leo Ouimet opened it in 1907 in Montreal. He charged 10 to 15 cents a seat, and 25 cents for reserved seats — those were luxury prices when nickelodeons were charging 5 cents (that's where the name *nickelodeon* comes from!).

A Pixillating Genius

Canada's National Film Board (NFB) is famous for its original and outstanding work. Norman McLaren was among the NFB's most original filmmakers. In 1941 the Board asked the young artist to set up an animation unit. McLaren experimented with drawing directly on film to create animation. He is best known for his award-winning use of stop-motion filming. Called pixillation, it's the technique that makes everyday objects seem to move by themselves. This creates lamps with personality and drivers who speed along roads without cars.

How is pixillation done? It's a time-consuming though ingenious technique. A movie camera is set to take a single frame at a time. Objects are set up. *Click!* Then the objects are moved a tiny distance. *Click* again! And so on, for hundreds of thousands of frames. The movers of the objects are never filmed, so the objects seem to move on their own. The only limit is the filmmaker's imagination.

If you can borrow a video camera, you can try it yourself. Hilarious scenes can unfold, with shoes walking by themselves, drawers opening and closing by themselves — anything you can plan and set up.

McLaren was the master. Filmmakers still use this form of animation, but another form has become even more powerful . . .

Computer Animation Born in Canada

In 1996 Nestor Burtnyk mounted a stage in Hollywood to accept his Academy Award from actress Helen Hunt. A talented actor? A director? No, Burtnyk was a researcher at the National Research Council (NRC) in Ottawa. He invented key frame computer animation technology — the first big breakthrough in computer animation of films.

Computers were room-sized, with limited memory, when Burtnyk started his research in 1967 at the NRC, where workers were building a graphics-display generator. In 1969 Burtnyk heard about the thousands of hand drawings required for animated movies at Disney Studios. He thought a computer could take over some of that work, and decided to make animation easier for creative artists. He would design computer software that would let computers generate smooth movements. The artists would retain all creative control, but wouldn't have to hand draw every frame.

With key frame animation, artists can draw the most important frames into the computer with a digitizing pen. Then they "tell" the computer the sequence of drawings in the scene. The computer can fill in the rest. Instant playback lets artists see the movements they are creating, so they can edit as they work. Later Burtnyk developed the "skeleton-driven" technique that lets the animator create motions using a control skeleton for each image part. "Tweening" and "morphing" computer packages were based on Burtnyk's innovations.

Computer animation is a multi-billion-dollar industry in Canada, and some of the best animators are trained here. When you see computer animated films, thank Burtnyk, whose twenty-eight years of work launched the art form. He shared his Academy Award with Marceli Wein of Kingston, who worked with him to develop the ideas behind computer animation.

Canadian Company Blazes
Computer Animation Trail

The very first television show in the world produced entirely with computer-generated imagery, *ReBoot*, was created by Mainframe Entertainment Inc., of Vancouver, British Columbia. An international team of animators, Ian Pearson, Phil Mitchell and Gavin Blair, worked out of a Vancouver hotel room in the beginning, giving birth to *ReBoot*.

Why did they come to Vancouver? "Well, our first reason for moving was because it was so beautiful, and the second was the wealth of animation talent in the city," explains Gavin Blair, co-creator of *ReBoot*. It was the early 1990s.

Their brainchild was slick, visually stunning and filled with jet-propelled action, sophisticated "camera" angles and effects, set inside a computer world called Mainframe. The show was a brilliant fantasy based on the very hardware and software Mainframe Entertainment used to create the series. The engagingly human characters of *ReBoot* faced annihilation on an epic scale as the mysterious User downloaded them into nightmarish computer games. Strong story lines drove the action, with lots of comic sidekick characters and spoofs of stories old and new.

When the series started, Bob, the blue-skinned Guardian program, and green-skinned Dot Matrix, were the main defenders of Mainframe City. Dot's little brother Enzo alternately helped and harried them. Set against them were the evil Megabyte virus and his sister, Hexadecimal, a masked queen who loved to spread chaos.

Computer-smart children and teens were ready for a show that seemed to leap out of computerland by itself — complete with computer puns — to challenge their imaginations. Software from Softimage helped the creators begin, but they had to develop new software to advance the technology of computer animation. A program called Grin allowed them to lip-synch the dialogue, for example. When ABC agreed to broadcast the show, the animators went into high gear to solve their software problems and create characters and background images.

Three years of development and three backers were needed before the series at last debuted in 1994. The show ran for three seasons. Since then it has spread to other networks and over 70 countries. In 2001 two feature-length made-for-TV movies brought back the hugely popular *ReBoot* gang.

Mainframe Entertainment has had nine computer animated shows on television since their ground-breaking early days, and produced more than 230 hours of computer animation. Along the way the company grew from fifteen people to over three hundred artists, animators, technicians and support staff, with earnings of $2.4 million in 2001. The company has picked up numerous awards, including four Geminis and an Emmy, and the Smithsonian Institution added some of their work to its collection in 1998.

Expect to see Canadian companies and Canadians at the forefront of future computer animation developments.

Winnie the Canadian Bear

Do you remember Winnie the Pooh? Most people do. International star of the British children's stories, Pooh bear was inspired by a real bear — a Canadian bear named after a Manitoba city. Perhaps no other bear has given as much joy to children around the world as this one has.

On August 24, 1914, Lt. Harry Colebourn of the 34th Fort Garry Horse Regiment of Manitoba left home to fight in World War I. During a brief train stop at White River, Ontario, he found an orphaned black bear cub on the station platform. Colebourn bought her for $20 and took her to England with him. He named the playful cub Winnie after his hometown, Winnipeg. She became the soldiers' pet. When Colebourn went to France to fight, he left Winnie in the care of the London Zoo, where he visited her whenever he could. He had always intended to bring her back to Canada with him, but Winnie had become a major attraction at the zoo. Visitors young and old came to love her.

In 1919 Colebourn gave Winnie to the London Zoo. There, author A. A. Milne and his son Christopher visited and came to love Winnie, too. In 1926 Milne created the Winnie the Pooh character inspired by her. Winnie lived at the London Zoo until her death on May 12, 1934.

Colebourn's love of animals led him to veterinary school in Guelph, Ontario. He practised as a vet in Winnipeg.

Saskatchewan artist William H. Epp created a sculpture of Colebourn and Winnie the bear in 1992. The sculpture stands in a park in Winnipeg, a reminder of Winnie. It is dedicated to the children of the world.

Canada's Favourite Game First Played at Home

Take a hard rubber puck and two teams wearing ice skates. Give them bent sticks to hit the puck, and nets to aim for — and stand well back. Shards of ice are about to fly, to say nothing of the puck itself, and, occasionally, teeth. Ice hockey is a fast, exhilarating sport, and Canadians' favourite game. The players have to be superb skaters, with deadly accurate aim and lots of competitive spirit. The fans sometimes yell so loudly the players can barely hear the referee's whistle. That's hockey, Canadian style.

No one is absolutely sure where ice hockey was born. What we do know is that "hockey" used to mean a field game played in England. Some indigenous people in North America actually played a hockey-like game they called *oomchankunutk*. The modern game of ice hockey might also have evolved from the Irish field game of hurley.

Windsor, Nova Scotia, has long claimed to be the birthplace of hockey, but the Society of International Hockey Research disagrees. What is Windsor's claim? A graduate of nearby King's College School dates the playing of hurley-on-ice to 1800. That graduate, Judge Thomas Chandler Haliburton, wrote some scenes in a novel based on his own experience of playing hurley at the back of the college grounds. He described "boys let out racin', yelpin', hollerin', and whoopin' like mad with pleasure . . . [playing] hurley on the long pond on the ice." After the game the boys hiked home through the woods, past Frog Pond and Devil's Punch Bowl, their other skating "rinks." The hurley puck itself was made of hardwood.

According to those who favour Windsor as hockey's birthplace, when the King's College students scattered to their far flung homes, from Halifax to England, they took their new sport with them. The popular game soon interfered with church attendance in Halifax. Clergy and parents were against it. Variously called hurley, wicket or ricket, the game was played by everyone from students to coal miners in those early days.

On Christmas Day, 1855, in Kingston, Ontario, soldiers played the game on the harbour ice. Members of the Royal Canadian Rifles cleared the snow, strapped blades to their boots, and borrowed field hockey sticks and a lacrosse ball. Field hockey rules were used, but the game was a far cry from that land sport. Skating added speed and risk to the game, and demanded highly skilled athletes. Better skates became available when John Forbes invented Spring Skates, which clamped onto boot soles and heels.

The Prince of Wales visited Halifax in 1860. Reports from 1863 claim he played ice hockey in England. Had he learned it in Canada? The Canadian sport was migrating faster than a snow goose.

James Creighton of Halifax taught the game to friends at McGill University in Montreal. Creighton also wrote the Halifax Rules for ice hockey, with nine players to a side. They used sticks sent from Halifax.

By 1893 the game had spread to nearly a hundred clubs in Montreal, and to places all over Canada and the United States. Lord Stanley, Canada's Governor General, left behind a hockey trophy, a sterling silver bowl bearing his name, when he returned to England that year. The Stanley Cup, now the oldest trophy in professional athletics in North America, was awarded to the Montreal Amateur Athletic Association by Lord Stanley before he left Canada. When the National Hockey League was formed in 1917, the trophy became its coveted award.

The first public exhibition game took place in Montreal in 1895. For the first time, spectators formally gathered to cheer and jeer. The future of the game looked very bright.

Where did hockey equipment originate? Early sticks had been handmade by the Mi'kmaq. In 1900 James Leggatt of Hamilton, Ontario, became the first to patent the two-piece hockey stick. Fishing nets had been thrown over the goal posts the year before in

Nova Scotia, and were tested in Toronto in 1900. Within a hundred years, the game of ice hockey as we know it had evolved. Two hundred years after hockey's crude beginnings, we still love the sport. When both Canadian men's and women's teams won Olympic Gold in 2002, the whole country cheered them on.

Safer Hockey

"He shoots! He scores! *Ouch!* The goalie took it in the face! He's down. Medics are on the ice . . . "

This scene was all too common in ice hockey matches until the widespread use of protective goalie face masks. A few goaltenders experimented with masks decades before the face mask would be accepted, including Montreal Maroons player Clint Benedict around 1930. But masks never caught on until Jacques Plante wore one. The modern hockey face mask has become standard protection for players of all ages, from kids' to professional teams, because of two Canadians. Today, fans collect pictures of the colourful, varied masks their favourite goalies wear.

By 1959, Jacques Plante, an NHL All-Star goalie, had been injured in the face many times. Fast-travelling pucks had broken his jaw, both cheekbones and his nose. He had already had 200 stitches in his face. He had even suffered a hairline fracture of the skull. Plante decided that was enough. He made his own rigid goalie mask, with some help from Fiberglas Canada.

Plante was afraid fans might think less of him for wearing a mask. And his coach opposed the mask, so at first he only wore it during practices. But after a puck gave him a big gash in his upper lip during a game, he refused to return to the ice without the mask. He proved it didn't interfere with his playing by winning the game. After that, Plante decided to wear it for every game. When his team, the Montreal Canadiens, won the Stanley Cup for the third time in a row, Plante was in the net and the mask was on.

Plante led the way by *wearing* his mask. Toronto-born Dr. Tom Pashby worked to *make* both the mask and helmets standard hockey equipment. A keen hockey fan, Pashby never missed a game at Toronto's Maple Leaf Gardens. His friend George Parsons was playing for the Leafs in 1939 when he took a hockey stick in the face and was blinded in one eye. The cause? Highsticking. Parsons lost both the eye and his hockey career that night.

Pashby had nearly finished medical school when he witnessed this gruesome accident, and he was shaken. He became an ophthalmologist, or eye doctor. Soon he was stitching up players after the games at the Gardens. His own son suffered a head injury during a house league hockey game, but recovered. After another player in the majors was blinded in 1973, the Canadian Ophthalmological Society knew who could help. Pashby prepared a report on the extent of eye injuries in hockey. It helped change hockey rules.

In 1975 the Canadian Amateur Hockey Association (CAHA) modified the highsticking rules, making the game safer. Pashby pushed the Canadian Standards Association (CSA) for rules on protective eyewear. By 1979 all minor hockey players had to wear a CSA-approved face-protector-and-helmet combination. It was the first safety standard like it anywhere. Eye injuries in hockey were cut dramatically.

Now, no one scoffs at a hockey player in a helmet, or a goalie with a helmet and face mask. And highsticking is not allowed. Canada led the way, and Pashby continued to push for eye protection in other sports.

One of the World's Most Popular Games

A game doesn't have to be complicated to require top athletic ability. Putting a ball through a hoop looks deceptively easy. It really requires a gifted eye, balance, outstanding aim and years of practice. To do it in a team setting, while other players do everything they can to stop you, takes the moves of a champion.

Canadian-born James Naismith, a physical education instructor at the YMCA in Springfield, Massachusetts, invented basketball in December of 1891. He wanted to make winter gymnasium exercises interesting and injury-free for the football players he coached. He needed a team game that required skill and fitness, but *no* body contact. Naismith had no idea that his game would become the world's leading indoor team sport.

Naismith remembered the "duck-on-a-rock" stone-throwing game of his Ontario childhood. He came up with thirteen rules and raised the "goals" 3 metres above ground, nailing half-bushel peach baskets to the balconies overlooking the gym, as targets. Finesse rather than force was required to throw the ball into the basket. Colleague Luther Gulick helped refine the game.

There was a glitch, though. Someone had to perch on a ladder to get the ball out of the basket and throw it back to the players. By sawing a hole in the bottom of the peach baskets, Naismith's assistant could poke the ball out of the basket with a broom. And the baskets could still be used for peaches later if a brace was put in the bottom of the used ones. Not until 1900 did a hoop with a net replace the baskets.

In 1936 men's basketball was recognized as an Olympic sport. The most famous early Canadian team was a crack group of women players, the Edmonton Commercial Grads, who won more than 500 of their 522 games. To this day, basketball, with its minimal equipment, remains an accessible game, loved by amateurs around the world. It has given rise to stars like Magic Johnston and Michael Jordan, teams like the Chicago Bulls and the Toronto Raptors.

Basketball reflects Naismith the man, with his rules for fair play. An outstanding athlete in numerous sports, Naismith knew about football injuries first-hand. He was a varsity football star, at McGill University and other institutions. He never missed a game for seven years. He also developed the football helmet — an invention that has undoubtedly saved lives — because he wanted to protect his often-injured ears. Naismith was a man of warmth and goodwill, who never patented his inventions to make money. "Let us all be able to lose gracefully and to win courteously," he once said, "[to] accept criticism as well as praise; and last of all, to appreciate the attitude of the other fellow at all times."

Jokester Pares Down the Game

Tommy Ryan was a Guelph-born practical joker, racehorse owner and Toronto businessman. He owned the classiest bowling alley in town, where businessmen came to bowl. At the time, bowling balls weighed over 7 kilograms and had to knock down ten pins each round — ten-pin bowling. Ryan invented five-pin bowling in 1908-09, a game of skill more than physical strength, a game whole families could enjoy. Over a million Canadians across the country play the game today.

In 1904 Ryan opened his bowling alley at 9 Temperance Avenue in Toronto's downtown business district. A string orchestra made music while the bowlers played. Occasionally Ryan's trick bow-tie sprayed the bowlers with a jet of water, but they seemed to take it as good fun. Business was good, but there was a problem. Lunch breaks were a half-hour in those days. Though businessmen flocked to the alley to play a game during their break, they complained that they couldn't finish a whole ten-pin game in that time. On top of that, the balls were heavy to lug to work, to the alley and back.

Ryan asked his father to pare down the heavy bowling pins to a smaller size on his wood lathe. Ryan provided smaller balls, too — 1.5 kilograms. He could afford to buy lots of the small balls, so no one would have to bring his own. And Ryan invented simplified scoring and playing rules.

There were still glitches to work out. The new pins scattered with a roar, often flying into other lanes or out the windows. It was hard to hear the orchestra, and pedestrians on the street below had to dodge falling pins. Pin boys had to dash around, trying to find the pins to reset them, until Ryan put thick rubber bands around the pins to control their scatter.

The new game boomed. Within a few years there were thirty-two bowling alleys in Toronto alone. Women and children soon joined in the fun, attracted by the lighter ball. Thomas Ryan never patented his invention, though. He was already wealthy — he just wanted to provide a good clean sport. His game took off across the country and the United States.

Rope Tow Gives Skiers a Lift

How often would you ski if you had to walk up the slope every time? Skiing has been around a lot longer than ski lifts and tows. Alex Foster invented and installed the first rope tow in the world in 1930 (or possibly 1931, according to some sources). He was a teenager at the time, from Sainte-Agathe-des-Monts, Quebec. Skiers with a sense of humour dubbed his invention Foster's Folly.

How did skiers get to the top of the hill *before* tows or lifts? Believe it or not, skiers in Quebec used to strap seal skins to the bottom of their skis to grip the snow on the uphill climb. Some lucky skiers got a tow holding on to a rope behind an automobile or a horse-drawn sleigh as it followed snow-covered roads to the upper slopes.

The Laurentian Lodge Club, formed in 1922, was already a famous skiing spot in the Laurentian Mountains north of Montreal. Foster was part of an award-winning McGill University ski team that practised there. He saw an opportunity to earn some money.

He created his rope tow by driving a stake into the ground at the top of Big Hill, the Club's favourite slope. At the bottom of the hill he parked an old Dodge, the local taxi he had rented for the weekend. He jacked it up on blocks, removed one of the back tires and used the wheel rim for power. A long loop of rope and a pulley completed the system. Foster attached the pulley to the stake at the hilltop, and passed the rope around the bare wheel rim. Then he started up the car, and Foster's Folly was in business. Hoisted on blocks, the taxi went nowhere fast. But the skiers had only to grab the rope to get towed up the hill as the loop revolved. First Foster charged 25 cents a ride, and then dropped his price to 25 cents for half a day.

Within two years Vermont skiers heard of the rope tow, and paid their innkeepers $75 to investigate it. The world's second rope tow, attached to a Model T Ford truck, was soon in place outside

Woodstock, Vermont. The idea spread quicker than a winter cold after that, and made skiing much more popular. The tough climb to the top of ski hills could be avoided, and more downhill runs could be packed into a day, so people were willing to pay the tow charge. By the mid-1940s, rope tows, T-bars and chairlifts were common on both Alpine and North American ski slopes.

Foster supervised the installation of other rope tows in the Laurentians, where a ski trail, Foster's Run, was named after him. An eccentric and gifted skier, he invented a way to turn full circles while coming downhill, a move called the Alex royale in his honour.

Queen of the Schooners

Sails ruled the seas for centuries. Harnessing only the power of the wind, sailing ships cut through the waves in all weather for fun and for profit. Among the fastest ever built were the schooners, used for fishing the Grand Banks off the eastern coast of Canada. And among these, Canada's *Bluenose* was the fastest fishing schooner ever built. Designed by Nova Scotia-born, self-taught naval architect William Roue in 1920-1921, she's a Canadian legend. She sails on the back of the Canadian 10-cent coin, an image of excellence and pride.

She was built to win back the International Fishermen's Trophy. Beginning in 1920, the *Halifax Herald* newspaper offered the trophy to the fastest deep-sea fishing ship. In that year's race, Nova Scotia's Lunenburg crew lost the trophy to the Gloucester, Massachusetts, entry. Lunenburg had been home to world-class fishing and ship-building since the 1700s. The two ports were rivals, famous for both deep-sea fishing and shipbuilding. Race entries for the trophy had to be working fishing schooners from these two ports.

Canadian pride had been wounded by the 1920 loss, so Roue was hired to build a faster working schooner. The result was the *Bluenose*. Halifax businessmen financed the $36,000 it cost to build her. She fished the Grand Banks after her March, 1921, launch, and then sailed to victory in that year's race. The International Fishermen's Trophy returned to Canada, and never left again.

In eighteen years of racing, the *Bluenose* continued to amaze sailors. Other American and Canadian vessels were built in an effort to surpass her, but none could equal her speed. During her last race in 1938 she averaged 14.15 knots, with a top speed of 16 knots (close to 23 kilometres per hour) — the fastest fishing schooner in the world. (Cruising speed for a sailing vessel is about 10 knots.)

In the *Bluenose,* Roue combined the breadth and depth of Nova Scotia fishing vessels with the clean lines of a racer. With a deck 44 metres long and a mainmast 38 metres tall, she could set 1,036 square metres of sail, to give her speed. Eighteen men crewed her, including a chief cook and five officers. William Roue designed 200 different ships and yachts in his lifetime, and his wealth of experience showed in the greatness of the *Bluenose.*

Angus Walters, skipper of the *Bluenose,* was forced to sell her in 1942 when fish prices fell too low to finance her and her crew. The West Indian Trading Company bought her and sailed her in the Caribbean until 1946, when she was wrecked. Said Walters of her construction, "I don't feel as there was a vessel that ever came out of Lunenburg that had sticks stepped that perfect."

Why was she called the *Bluenose*? Two possible reasons — for the blue-skinned potatoes shipped from Nova Scotia to Boston beginning in the 1780s, or for the blue-coloured noses of small-craft fishermen on the cold North Atlantic.

With Angus Walters's consent, a replica of the *Bluenose* was built in 1963, financed by the Olands Brewery to promote their Schooner beer. The masts and deck are of Douglas fir, the hull of red oak, spruce and pine; the sails of Dacron. In 1972 Olands turned the *Bluenose II* over to the province of Nova Scotia. The original *Bluenose* had often taken school children and members of the public on board for goodwill tours, and the province continued that tradition.

In 1995 *Bluenose II* needed extensive rebuilding to keep her seaworthy, so the *Bluenose II* Preservation Trust, a non-profit group of volunteers working out of the Fisheries Museum of the Atlantic in Lunenburg, took on the task. Today young men and women can crew the *Bluenose II* under professional guidance and learn the challenges and thrills of Canada's sailing heritage.

Canadian STOLs Lead the World

Imagine a vast trackless wilderness dotted with countless lakes and rivers. Imagine forests, swamps, rocky hills and muskeg, frozen for months at a time. That's the Canadian North — beautiful beyond words, but sometimes a traveller's nightmare, with an abundance of pristine places to swim, camp, hunt, fish or look for minerals . . . and no way to get there, except maybe by canoe. Because it could land on frozen muskeg or on a lake, the bush plane opened up the North.

A brilliant innovation, the bush plane made it possible to get people and cargoes in and out of remote parts of the North. De Havilland Canada designed and built the first bush plane in 1947 for bush pilots and the military, and called it the Beaver. The Beaver was the world's first true short takeoff and landing plane (STOL), and many people consider the tough and versatile plane the world's best bush aircraft. It was so well designed and made that the first 1947 prototype was still flying in 1980 when the Canadian Aviation Museum bought it for display.

The Beaver was a huge success. About 60 countries outside Canada ordered it for both domestic and military uses. After it won United States Air Force and Army competitions for utility aircraft in 1951, the U.S. military bought nearly a thousand of the tough little plane. While in service during the Korean War it was dubbed the "general's jeep." More Beavers were built than any other Canadian-made and Canadian-designed aircraft — a remarkable 1,600 planes.

What made the Beaver so special? It could land on very short runways on wheels, skis or pontoons. It could climb at a rate of 311 metres per minute, even with a heavy load of about 900 kilograms — crucial for getting in and out of tight spots. With all-metal construction and a high lift wing 14.6 metres long, the robust Beaver had a range of 756 kilometres. Powered by one Pratt & Whitney Wasp 450-horsepower engine, it was quieter than standard aircraft, too. The Beaver was the practical workhorse of pilots in rough territory, delivering cargo and people to places without runways.

Soon people wanted a plane with all the advantages of the Beaver, but faster and bigger. De Havilland came up with the more powerful Turbo-Beaver, and with the larger Otter and Twin Otter, Caribou and Buffalo, as newer light engines became available. The Canadian planes were part of a demonstration of landing and taking off from downtown New York City in 1966, where they dramatically showed off their STOL capabilities. Suddenly, it was possible to have downtown airports and short commuter flights.

Twice the size of the Beaver, the Otter could land on a strip only 300 metres long, and carry nine passengers plus the two-person crew. Beginning in 1951 the Otter served the Ontario Provincial Air Service, the RCAF, Canadian airlines, the U.S. Navy, the United Nations Emergency Force in the Middle East, and parts of Norway. An impressive record! It even flew in the Antarctic.

The Twin Otter was the enlarged twin-engine version of the Otter. Over a period of twenty-two years, three versions of this plane were produced — a total of 844 aircraft. Twin Otters were sold to buyers around the world for use in jungles, deserts, mountains and the Arctic. There, their large balloon-like tires (called tundra tires) made landing on soft ground possible, so there was no need for a proper landing strip, even during the Arctic summer thaw.

With a twenty-passenger capacity, and the increased safety and reliability of twin engines, Twin Otters sell today at values up to twenty times their original price tags. Sturdy and long-lived, de Havilland's aircraft still wing through the world's skies.

Conquering Winter Isolation

In a small town in Quebec, in the depths of the winter, young Yvon Bombardier doubled over in pain. It was the mid-1930s. The two-year-old boy was dangerously ill. His father Joseph-Armand knew that Yvon needed hospital treatment, but the nearest hospital was 50 kilometres away in Sherbrooke, and the roads were blocked by huge snowdrifts. No sleigh, car or truck could travel through so much snow. In his garage Bombardier had an unfinished invention — a snowmobile. It could have carried his son to help, but he hadn't yet solved all the design problems. Yvon died of appendicitis.

The tragedy gave Bombardier new determination. He produced the B7 the following year, an emergency snowmobile with room for seven people inside its plywood cabin. It was driven by a rubber-cushioned drive wheel and track, and could travel over snow that stopped all other vehicles. Bombardier received the patent for his "auto-neige" in 1937 and began filling orders. These first large snowmobiles were used as buses, ambulances and emergency winter police vehicles. During World War II, Bombardier supplied the Canadian armed forces with snowmobiles that could carry up to twelve people.

Born in Valcourt, Quebec, in 1907, Bombardier started making machines early. When he was a boy he constructed his own moving toys out of cigar boxes and parts of clockworks, sewing machines and motors. His father gave him a worn-out car and a garage where he could tinker. At fifteen Bombardier decided to make a machine that could travel over winter snowfalls. He got his brother to help him. They removed the motor from the old car, mounted it on sleigh runners, attached a wooden propeller and produced the first motorized snowmobile. It terrorized townsfolk with its loud motor, but it worked. When neighbours demanded he shut down his invention, Bombardier decided to build a better machine. He wanted to end winter isolation.

Trained as a car mechanic, Bombardier opened a garage where he repaired anything brought to him. He was nineteen years old, and already a clever and innovative businessman. He astonished people with his flair for fixing machines. He even built a dam and turbine to generate electricity from the stream by his garage. And he continued to work on his snowmobile. In the 1930s and 1940s, engines were too heavy for a light, two-person model, but at last smaller air-cooled engines were available, enabling Bombardier to create the Ski-Doo in 1959. It was a smaller, lighter machine than his first creation, similar to today's models. First he called it the Ski Dog, but a typo changed the name, and he stuck with the new one.

The world's first commercially successful snowmobile, the Ski-Doo is a versatile machine. It can cross not just snowy, but soft, muddy, trackless terrain. It has been used in Holland to help build dikes, in Scotland to lay pipelines, in Peru to handle logs near the Amazon, in

Central American coffee plantations to reach inaccessible areas, and in Lapland to round up reindeer! In the Canadian North it offers an alternative to sled dogs. Riding it is a favourite winter sport, too.

Today Bombardier Incorporated has sold its millionth Ski-Doo and become a world-leading company. Bombardier Inc. designs and makes other transportation equipment such as subway trains and aerospace technologies. Joseph-Armand Bombardier was granted more than forty patents in his life, and his company has continued to flourish after his death.

The first Canadian to reach the North Pole by snowmobile was Bombardier's nephew, Jean-Luc Bombardier.

Aviation History's Premier Invention

The world's aircraft industry was made possible by the most important invention in the history of aviation — the variable-pitch propeller. Wallace Rupert Turnbull created it, and while other countries rushed to perfect the invention, Turnbull made the first variable-pitch propeller powered aircraft to fly successfully.

Born in St. John, New Brunswick, Turnbull observed various aircraft limitations and problems during World War I. He created the new propeller in 1916 in England, and brought it back to Canada in 1918.

Before Turnbull's invention, aircraft could fly, but they could not carry much of a load. Aviation progress was stalled. Aircraft really needed two different propeller designs — one to help power a plane into the air on takeoff, and a less powerful one that wouldn't waste energy when cruising along in the sky. But switching propellers in mid-air was clearly impossible, so Turnbull invented a new propeller with blades that could be adjusted to cut through the air at a different angle or pitch. A small electric motor changed the propellers' slant. With higher-pitched propeller blades, planes flew more efficiently during the long-distance portions of the flight, so they could carry more paying customers and cargo. The prop only needed to be at maximum power for takeoff and landing.

Turnbull's variable-pitch propeller won the silver medal at the New York Inventions Show in 1923, but later ground tests conducted at Camp Borden, Ontario, showed him that he had more work to do. His second design performed much better when it was flight tested there in 1927. By 1929 the variable-pitch propeller had proven itself.

Although Turnbull sold the rights to the variable-pitch prop to the Curtis-Wright Manufacturing Company of the United States and England's Bristol Aeroplane Company, he continued to test and invent devices in Rothesay, New Brunswick. To work on new wing designs he built the first wind tunnel ever made, and to test propellers he created a miniature railway. There, propellers powered test vehicles along the tracks — a safe way of testing that didn't involve actually being airborne.

After Alexander Graham Bell, Turnbull was perhaps the most prolific and successful private inventor in Canadian history — that is, one not connected with a major research institute. Like Bell, his contribution changed history.

Snow Removal, the Canadian Way

Deep snowfalls and drifts make winter travel in Canada tough. While Joseph-Armand Bombardier invented a way to travel *over* the snow, other inventors worked on clearing it *away*.

Until 1885, trains used a plow shaped like a wedge to cut through snow. When the snow was very deep or heavy, men had to get out and shovel it. Trains sat and waited for human muscles to dig them out, until better ways to clear train tracks were invented. Toronto dentist John W. Elliott patented a "compound revolving snow shovel" for trains in 1869, then "An Improvement on a Machine for Removing Snow from Railway Tracks" a year later. But railways did not adopt his idea right away.

In the 1880s, Orange Jull of Orangeville, Ontario, improved Elliott's model. Then Edward Leslie and his brother saw Jull's design and built a working model in their machine shop. In test trials the new machine threw snow 60 metres. But creating a full-sized steam-powered rotary prototype of the snowplow was beyond the capability of the Leslies' shop, so they had a New Jersey firm build it. Tests in 1885-86 were highly successful. Union Pacific Railway representatives were so impressed they purchased the prototype on

the spot and put in an order for three more. Canadian Pacific Railway had eight machines constructed in their Montreal shops. Finally, in 1911, thick armour-plated blades were added to handle heavy, wet snow and debris from mountain slides. Diesel-powered descendants of the rotary snowplow are still used today to clear avalanches and heavy snow from mountain tracks.

One man found a better way to clear roads, too. Arthur Sicard of Montreal, Quebec, invented the snowblower. With the machine, snow removal was fast and easy. Sicard sold his first working prototype to the town of Outremont in 1927.

Sicard cared about snow removal. He grew up on a Quebec farm, where he struggled through snow each winter to milk the cows. If a large snowdrift blocked his way to the market in Montreal, his horse and wagon couldn't get through, and the day's work was wasted. Sicard got the idea for the snowblower while watching a thresher harvest wheat in the fields. It used rotating blades to cut the wheat. Sicard's first attempt at a snowblower used the same principles. It worked well until it hit huge drifts. Then it bogged down.

Sicard could not raise sufficient funds to improve his invention. His neighbours thought he was a crackpot — who else would try to fight winter? So Sicard raised the money himself. He worked in Montreal as a construction labourer and road contractor, and saved his wages. By 1925 he had created a four-wheel-drive truck adapted to be a snowblower. The blades in front sent snow flying through an ejection chute. Sicard ran it in Montreal, and changed snow clearing forever. He had even thought about snow collection. His creation could throw the snow more than 30 metres away, or directly into a dump truck.

Quebec towns and cities were the first to buy snowblowers, then Ottawa's Department of Transport followed. Later, airports in Switzerland, and eventually, roads the world over, were being cleared of snow by Sicard's invention.

Hydrofoils: Ships with Wings

Hydrofoils skim the water on blades, reaching high speeds because they travel *above* the water.

Alexander Graham Bell started experimenting with hydrofoils around 1900. He created the first truly successful one, called the *Dhonnas Beag* (Little Devil), with Casey Baldwin in 1908 in Nova Scotia. The idea wasn't new, but no one had made a good working model before. For months Bell and Baldwin changed the boat's design, over and over, until they came up with the best one — essentially the same design as that used today.

The key was a set of "wings" under the water, on the boat's hull. They looked like rigid curved blades. As the boat's speed increased, the wings or hydrofoils lifted most of the boat's hull out of the water. Less contact with the water means less resistance, so higher speeds are possible.

The size and weight of motors of the time slowed Bell and Baldwin's research. In 1919 lighter aircraft engines allowed them to create the HD-4, which reached speeds of over 113 kilometres per hour, a world water-speed record that stood until 1930. Bell did not continue his research, but others, including the Canadian Navy, took up where he left off. Hydrofoils are still in use today.

On the Road from Sea to Sea

Walk, drive, roll or cycle — in Canada you can do it from coast to coast, from the Atlantic to the Pacific Oceans, across our enormous country. The longest national highway in the world is the Trans-Canada — a ribbon of asphalt 7,821 kilometres long. It spans the whole continent. Travelling it takes ten long days of non-stop driving, or two weeks with normal sleep breaks. If travellers stop to see anything along the way, the trip takes much longer — and there's a lot to see.

The Trans-Canada connects St. John's, Newfoundland, on the Atlantic Ocean to Victoria, British Columbia, on the Pacific, with the aid of two ferry rides. A vital artery for transportation, the Highway runs through barrens, forests, picturesque fishing villages and farmlands, past mines, lakes and bustling cities, through seas of wheat and spectacular mountain ranges. Canada is vast, spread over 9.9 million square kilometres, second in size only to Russia. Our population is small in comparison to our size, so connections between far-flung centres of population are crucial.

The making of the Trans-Canada took decades of staggering work. Continent-wide cooperation was needed. The Trans-Canada Highway Act was given Royal Assent on December 10, 1949. Then the federal government negotiated with each province to do its part. Each section of the construction had to be separately funded. Engineers blasted through bedrock. They crossed rivers and valleys with scores of bridges. They forged a path through trackless forests, around lakes great and small. They laid firm foundations through treacherous swamps and muskeg. The last section of the highway, from Fort Frances to Atikokan, Ontario, was opened on June 28, 1965. The completed Trans-Canada is a wonder of engineering know-how, and determination.

Millions of Canadians and visitors travel the Trans-Canada Highway to see the rugged wilderness, fertile farms and rich heritage embedded in the Canadian identity. That's one way to appreciate the Highway and the size of this country, from sea to shining sea.

The World's Longest Street

Now a bustling street at the heart of the city of Toronto, Yonge Street runs all the way from Toronto's harbour to distant Rainy River,

Ontario — 1,896 kilometres north and west. Also known as Highway 11, Yonge Street passes through forests, towns and cities, north to North Bay, then veers toward Thunder Bay at the head of Lake Superior, and finally heads straight west to the Manitoba border. The oldest part of Yonge Street was cleared by hand, pick and shovel more than a hundred years ago. Horses were used to drag away the trees felled to make way for it.

The first stretch — originally an 8.5-metre-wide road from York, now Toronto, north to Lake Simcoe — was surveyed for the military in 1793 and named for Sir George Yonge, British Secretary of War. Sir John Graves Simcoe, Governor of Upper Canada and founder of Toronto, ordered the road built to aid the army in case the Americans to the south invaded. Simcoe promised 200 acres (over 80 hectares) of land to settlers coming to live in muddy York. Each settler had to promise to clear 5 acres (almost 2.5 hectares) of land in every hundred acres, within twelve months, including a quarter-mile section of road in front of their property. Property owners along Yonge Street shared in clearing it by cutting down trees. Convicted drunks helped by removing tree stumps from Yonge Street as part of their sentence. The road from York to Lake Simcoe was passable by 1816.

By the mid-1800s Yonge Street had become the main route for traders, farmers and stagecoaches entering and leaving town. Timothy Eaton opened his first Toronto department store at 178 Yonge Street in the late 1860s. Other merchants followed, but they avoided the Dundas to College section of Yonge Street in what was called "the ward," where immigrants crowded the poor homes and businesses. Yonge Street became *the* place to shop by the 1900s. Estates replaced the surrounding forests, and cross-streets were named after the wealthy landowners who lived along the street. By 1939 there was a tavern district with a bad reputation. At one time Potter's Field Cemetery (since moved) lay just outside a tollgate to the north of the city. A rope and pulley helped vehicles climb a steep hill beyond. Coach travellers rested or changed horses at Montgomery's Inn further north.

Today Yonge Street has multiple personalities — recreational, cultural and residential at the harbourfront, followed by world class theatres, Toronto's Hockey Hall of Fame, and one of the world's busiest indoor shopping complexes, the Eaton Centre. The Centre rubs shoulders with tacky neon-lit stores in the downtown Toronto strip. As Yonge continues north, trendy boutiques, antique shops, cafés and apartments eventually give way to Mount Pleasant Cemetery, where many famous Canadians are buried. Further north there are skyscraper business buildings, and then strip malls.

Later extensions of Yonge Street were fuelled by the rush for gold, silver and nickel in mines north of the Great Lakes. In rugged Canadian Shield country, the soil has been scraped from the fantastic granite cliffs and the swampy homelands of moose, deer, beaver and wolf. There the road can run for kilometres without a sign of human life. Lone gas stations, and bus and train stops, dot the way. The train lines follow the highway much of the way.

The trails the highway follows were blazed by indigenous people long before Europeans came to challenge the wilderness and the black flies. Could anything contrast more with the teeming crowds of Canada's biggest city at the south end of the world's longest street?

* It would cost over $2,000 to take a cab from one end of Yonge Street to the other.

* In 1992, when the Toronto Blue Jays became the first Canadian team to win the World Series, over a million people poured onto Yonge Street for night-long celebrations. No incidents were reported to the police. Canadian, eh?

Inside a T. Rex Mouth

Drumheller's giant *T. rex* is four times bigger than the real-life dinosaur that ruled this part of Canada 70 million years ago, but just as good looking. Eight to twelve people at a time can climb the 106 stairs inside the body of the sculpture to stand in the mouth and look out from between the gigantic 30- to 60-centimetre-long teeth. Blink and you might imagine the roar of the hungry *T. rex*, the terrified honks of fleeing hadrosaurs, the buzz of biting insects. You might brace yourself for the chomp of those vicious teeth.

In Drumheller, Alberta, the world's largest dinosaur replica — a life-like *Tyrannosaurus rex* with attitude — stands about 25 metres high and 46 metres long. Care was taken to make the outside of the dinosaur realistic, right down to the claws and teeth. They reflect the latest dinosaur research. Amusement Leisure Worldwide constructed this giant replica from over 65 tonnes of steel, concrete and fibreglass. It opened in October, 2000, and hundreds of thousands of people have climbed it since then. Drumheller Regional Chamber of Development and Tourism built the *T. rex* as a non-profit millennium project, raising a million dollars from government and private funds to cover the costs. It commemorates Alberta's famous dinosaur bone and fossil sites, many of them along the nearby Red Deer River valley.

A two-hour drive south lies Drumheller Dinosaur Provincial Park, one of the richest fossil beds in the world. The United Nations

has named it a World Heritage Site. There, fossil finds record thirty-five dinosaur species, as well as nearly 300 species of plants and animals.

It Towers Above the World

You can get as dizzy looking up at it as you can if you're in the swiftly moving glass elevator. The world's tallest building (according to *The Guinness Book of World Records*) is the CN Tower in Toronto, Ontario. It soars to 553.33 metres at the tip of its antenna. That's as tall as five and a half football fields stacked end to end. Designed by John Andrews Architects and Webb Zerafa Menkes Housden Architects and NCK Engineering, the Tower is one of the wonders of the modern world. Made mainly of steel, concrete and glass, it weighs 117,910 tonnes.

Canadian National Railway (CNRail) began building the Tower in 1973, chiefly as a telecommunications centre and a symbol of the strength of Canadian industry. Another reason was that TV and radio signals were getting distorted by Toronto's tall buildings — a taller antenna was needed. From the Tower's telecommunications

centre, all major Toronto television and FM radio stations now broadcast, and reception in Toronto and surrounding areas is clear.

The CN Tower took forty months to construct and cost $63 million. A total of 1,537 courageous people built it, many of them working at dizzying heights. Crews worked twenty-four hours a day, five days a week.

The Tower is so high that the giant construction crane used to build the main structure had to be removed from it and the antenna lifted into place, section by section, by a powerful Sikorsky helicopter that weighed over 10 tonnes. Nicknamed "Olga," the helicopter worked for three and a half weeks to finish the job. Disaster nearly struck as Olga's job began, when the giant crane lurched as the helicopter tried to remove the first piece of its boom. The supporting bolts seized, the boom would not come loose . . . and Olga was *attached* to the boom with only fifty minutes of fuel remaining. With the operator still inside the crane, the lives of both the helicopter crew and the crane operator were at risk. Steelworkers quickly climbed the crane to burn the bolts off the boom, while Olga hovered, using up precious fuel. At last the bolts were cut and the helicopter lifted the crane to safety, landing with only fourteen minutes of fuel to spare. The rest of the job went smoothly. High-steel worker Paul Mitchell attached the last piece of antenna to the world's highest building.

The Tower has become a major tourist attraction, with 2 million people from all over the world visiting it each year. At its base are displays, motion simulator rides, films, arcades and other attractions. Visitors can travel up one of six glass-fronted, high-speed elevators at 22 kilometres per hour to reach the Look Out level at 346 metres. One level lower, they can stand on a specially designed glass floor and look down to the base of the Tower, far below. The Tower's 360 Restaurant, which revolves once every seventy-two minutes, has the most spectacular view in town. Another thirty-three storeys up, reached by a separate elevator, is the Sky Pod, with its amazing 360-degree view. On a windy day the Sky Pod sways more than a metre from the centre, but the building has been designed to safely sway that much around its hollow core, through winds of up to 193 kilometres per hour. The Tower can also withstand an earthquake of 8.5 on the Richter scale.

Lightning hits the CN Tower about thirty times a year, more than anywhere else in Toronto, but the electricity is safely carried to the ground by forty-two rods. Because the Tower is so high, a light at the top of the structure alerts aircraft to its presence.

During two events held each year, thousands of people climb the Tower's stairway — the world's longest — to raise over $1 million for charities. The climb has been done on pogo stick and motorcycle, and by people carrying a piano . . . even people carrying a dismantled car, or riding in a wheelchair. In 1989 Brendan Keenoy set the world record by climbing the 1,760 steps in 7 minutes and 52 seconds!

S-s-snakes Galore!

On warm days in May they make their way to the sunshine, a living carpet of red and black, their scales whispering as they rustle over and under each other. They have not eaten during winter hibernation, and have lost up to one third of their body weight. But still, mating comes first. As many as a hundred smaller males will entwine the larger females as they emerge from the den into the pit — an amazing slithery sight. Afterward the females head for a bog to eat frogs, insects and fish, and to raise their young. Unlike most of their kind, the females won't lay eggs, but will bear their young live. The males play no part in raising young, but will follow.

The world's largest snake dens are in the Narcisse Wildlife Management Area, near Inwood, Manitoba. No other reptiles in the world thrive so far north. Astonished scientists come from far and wide to study them, but no one knows why so many snakes settled into their northern Manitoba home.

The red-sided garter snakes are not dangerous, just awesome. The females can reach over a metre in length; the males are smaller. Thousands make their winter dens in deep limestone crevices and caves that are 10,000 years old. Each spring they leave their dens to stream to nearby bogs and marshes. They return in the fall. It's safe to touch them then — you can gently pick one up and allow it to slither freely from hand to hand. (Usually they will not bite, but if they do, it is not poisonous.) But leave them alone in the spring, at mating time. If you bother them then, they won't reproduce.

These harmless and beautiful snakes are sometimes clubbed to death, burned or sold off by snake pickers. And too many of the bogs they call home have been drained. Snakes are protected by law in the Narcisse Wildlife Management Area, but these natural wonders of the world are in trouble. They are being killed by floods, overharvesting, interference and destruction of their habitat.

To highlight this natural wonder, local artists Marlene Hour and Graham and Nera Clarke made s-s-sensational s-s-snake s-s-sculptures of S-s-sam and S-s-sara, 8 and 9 metres in length, made of rebar, polyurethane foam, metal lath and fibreglass. Volunteers raised the funds to create the romantic pair.

World's Tallest Totem Pole

In 1973 a totem pole 53 metres tall was raised in Alert Bay, British Columbia, becoming the world's tallest. The pole, made of only two giant logs, is a stunning feat of carving. Every part of it is full of meaning.

It rises at the north end of Cormorant Island on the outskirts of the village of Alert Bay. There it depicts the totems of some of the West Coast Kwakwaka'wakw tribes of the Namgis First Nation. The totem pole was carved in the late 1960s by Jimmy Dick, assisted by Benjamin, Adam and William Dick, Gus Matilpi and Mrs. Billy Cook, all Namgis First Nation artists. From the top down the stylized figures represent Sun Man, Kolus (Thunderbird's cousin), Whale, Old Man, Wolf, Thunderbird, Dzunuk'wa (wild woman of the woods who steals and eats bad children), Sisiul (double-headed sea serpent), Bear Holding a Salmon, Raven and finally another Dzunuk'wa holding a Copper (a thin, shield-shaped copper piece usually covered with pictures of important events in the owner's life; traditionally the Copper represented a person's wealth).

Every figure on the pole lives in the stories, beliefs and legends of the

Namgis First Nation. For example, the Salmon is a symbol of the First People's pride in their land. And it was said that if you looked a Sisiul in the eye you would turn to stone, but a glance at it out of the corner of your eye brought luck. However, everlasting poison would remain on the spear tip of any young warrior who succeeded in killing the serpent.

What are totem poles for? Families of some First Nations peoples have totem animals or spirit creatures. These totems are carved into a totem pole's wood, to recount the family history of those having the pole erected. Other carvings tell of the family's ceremonial privileges. In earlier times, whenever a totem pole was erected, a potlatch was usually held. During the potlatch the host would give away all his goods to his guests. Stories relating to the carvings on the totem pole were told at the potlatch celebration and feast. Seventeen unique totem poles, dating from 1870 on, stand watch over the sacred Burial Grounds in Alert Bay.

Monster Shopping Centre Holds World Records

The world's largest entertainment and shopping centre is the West Edmonton Mall, in — where else? — Edmonton, Alberta. A strange place for the biggest mall on the globe? Ask the more than 22 million people a year who visit it. With 20 hectares of enclosed climate-controlled shopping, eating and amusements, the mall is spread over a site the equivalent of forty-eight city blocks. Construction started in 1981 and cost $1.2 billion, with expansions in '83, '85 and '98.

What brings so many people to visit the place? Its creators included something for every member of the family. It contains over 800 stores and services, including a hotel, a lake, a skating rink, a ship, restaurants, a bowling alley and a miniature golf course.

The mall is the holder of seven world records. It houses the world's biggest indoor amusement park, Galaxyland, containing the Mindbender, a fourteen-storey roller coaster that's the highest triple-loop coaster in the world. For those seeking other adrenaline boosts, there are the Rock 'n' Wall, or the Centre of Gravity Bungee Jump.

In the world's largest indoor water park, visitors can swim, slide and splash in the world's largest indoor wave pool. Even the coldest winter day is a good day for swimming. This is definitely part of the mall's appeal in a part of Canada where the winters are long and the summer days can be swelteringly hot.

For non-swimmers, four seaworthy submarines cruise the world's largest indoor man-made lake, giving riders a fish-eye view of 200 species of marine life. Visitors can touch tidal pool species or even see living penguins. Students can watch in-depth views of the aquariums, plus educational presentations. Dolphin shows take place next to an exact replica of the *Santa Maria*, Christopher Columbus's ship.

The Edmonton Oilers practise in the NHL-sized ice arena, but public skating times are available too. There are twenty-six movie theatre screens, a Las Vegas-style casino, a bingo hall, a comedy club, a dinner theatre and Mardi Gras style entertainments. Foods for every taste are provided in restaurants and food courts. The mall even presents night-long Rock 'n' Ride Dance Parties for teens nine times a year, with access to Galaxyland rides.

So many attractions, but what about the parking? For that there's the world's largest parking lot, with 20,000 spaces. Over 23,500 employees are needed to operate the world's largest mall.

Giant Trilobite Dwarfs All Others

To picture it, imagine a huge bug twice as big as a house cat, covered by a flat hard shell. The eyes are on the top. Beneath the armoured shell, imagine numerous jointed legs and a mouth to match its size. Now be glad you're not swimming in the water with it! Just a fossil now, this creature is still an amazing giant — the world's largest known complete trilobite fossil. A spectacular 72 centimetres in length, it is a full 30 centimetres bigger than past finds.

This giant trilobite ruled the seas 445 million years ago. Canadian scientists discovered its remains on a rocky shoreline near Churchill, in northern Manitoba, in 1998. No one knows why the trilobites grew so big in this area.

Paleontologist Dave Rudkin found the massive specimen on a fossil-hunting expedition. Rudkin studies trilobites, and recognized the huge tail sticking out of the layers of rock. He said, "If more of it is here, this could be the biggest trilobite anywhere." It was. Expedition members painstakingly chipped away the limestone to free the giant trilobite and carry it to the Manitoba Museum. Seldom do paleontologists studying ancient sea creatures get such a thrill — usually trilobite fossils are between 3 and 10 centimetres long.

Trilobites lived in the coastal waters near Churchill, in what is now the subarctic. But 445 million years ago it was a tropical region. The local seas were teeming with life then — a previous fossilized specimen, 43 centimetres long, was found in the same area. Trilobites died out about 250 million years ago, but very distant relatives — crabs, scorpions and insects — survive today.

The giant is now housed at the Manitoba Museum in Winnipeg. Says Associate Curator Graham Young, it "illustrates some of the diversity and weirdness of ancient life."

You Can't Spend This Nickel!

Most Canadian coins are made of nickel, but only the 5-cent piece has the popular name of "nickel." The world's largest nickel, a giant 9-metre replica of the 1951 Canadian coin, can be found in Sudbury. In exact detail it reproduces the face of King George VI on one side (7 metres wide!), and a stylized nickel foundry and maple leaves on the reverse. Like the original nickel, it even has 244 dots along the edge. (Until the 2001 version, all Canadian nickels had these dots.)

The Big Nickel weighs over 18 tonnes and is 61 centimetres thick. It was built from 8 tonnes of stainless steel (the nickel in it is what makes the steel stainless) and lead backing, and over 10 tonnes of angle-iron framework. The coin was a private project to commemorate Canada's 1967 Centennial.

The nickel was a natural choice for Sudbury, Ontario. The monument is a tribute to the men and women who mine and process nickel in the Sudbury Basin. Sixty kilometres long and 27 kilometres wide, the Basin was formed by a meteor strike so powerful it formed cracks that let liquid rock stream up to the earth's surface from deep underground. The lava mixed with pre-existing rocks, allowing the formation of nickel ore. The ore deposits are being used up, but Canada remains a world leader in nickel production. Inco Ltd. fills a quarter of the world's demand, second in world production after Russia's Norilsk Nickel. Canada's Falconbridge Ltd. is third among nickel producers. Stainless steel, car parts and girders owe their strength and corrosion resistance to nickel.

The Big Nickel has brought visitors from around the world to Sudbury. Unveiled in July, 1967, and placed atop a 4-metre-high base on a hill overlooking Sudbury and the mines, it was the showpiece of the world's only numismatic park, along with several other giant replica coins. Visitors toured an underground mine, rode a model railroad and explored a half-scale replica of the lunar landing module, too.

The entire Big Nickel Project was the brainchild of Ted Szilva, a Sudbury firefighter. He suggested it as Sudbury's centennial project. When his proposal was rejected, Szilva decided to build it himself. He bought the project site for a $25 down payment, and sold Big Nickel medallions by mail order to finance it. Collectors from over 81 countries bought them. Artist Bruno Cavallo designed the monument and his workshop constructed it at a cost of $35,000.

Now owned by Science North, the replica sits next to this world class interactive science centre in Sudbury.

World's Biggest Rodeo

Take your courage when you go, because it's hair-raising just to watch what the cowhands do at the Calgary Stampede. And they do it all without a safety belt.

The Calgary Stampede hosts the world's biggest rodeo, where contestants compete for millions of dollars in prizes. The main events have their roots in the hard and dangerous work needed to manage cattle ranches in the days of the Wild West. Back then, a few people with horses had to control hundreds of cattle on the open range. They needed strength, agility, know-how and daring to do their jobs. They herded cattle, roped them, branded them and protected the herd. The only way to manage cattle was from the back of a horse, so cowhands developed amazing horseback-riding and cattle-related skills. This rodeo is the Olympics of cowboy sports.

The main outdoor events are bareback bronc riding, saddle bronc riding, bull riding, calf roping and steer wrestling. Staying on the back of a bucking horse or bull longer than seems humanly possible before being thrown close to its thundering hooves, or bringing down a steer with no more than a rope, willpower and brawn, are death-defying acts. Then there's wild-cow milking and wild-horse racing. The competitors are elite athletes who risk life and limb in their daredevil stunts. So do the clowns, even though they also get the crowd laughing, a good break between thrills and chills. Other activities, like the chuckwagon races, are straight out of pioneer days, when a wagon was the travelling kitchen for cowhands driving huge herds long distances to market.

The first Calgary Stampede was held in 1912, at a cost of $100,000. Today, millions of visitors from around the world flock to Calgary for the Stampede. It isn't just a rodeo. A midway, concerts, parades and parties go on for ten days. Visitors can see an authentic First Peoples village and a re-created frontier town. There are animal and agricultural events and exhibits, too.

Tidal Power

In some places the tide washes in gently twice a day, its rise and fall hardly noticed. But not in the Bay of Fundy. The world's largest tides run in this bay separating Nova Scotia from New Brunswick. So strong is the tide that it reverses the flow of rivers emptying into the Bay. Twice a day seawater runs in tidal bores *up* the riverbeds of the Bay of Fundy as high tide comes in. This creates the famous Reversing Falls on the Saint John River — rapids that change direction. High tide in the Minas Basin, one of the narrowest parts of the Bay of Fundy, runs to over 16 metres near Wolfville, Nova Scotia. That's the height of a five-storey building! At low tide, boats that were floating dockside end up on dry seabed far below.

The weight of the tidal waters is 14 billion tonnes. So heavy is this vast flow that the whole of Nova Scotia tilts slightly under the enormous load of water.

Why are the tides so extreme? The shape and depth of the Bay of Fundy funnels the powerful tides of the Atlantic Ocean. As the Bay narrows, the flow runs faster and rises higher.

The tidal flow is put to work at the Annapolis Basin on Nova Scotia's coastline. Tidal waters are trapped at high tide and allowed to flow through a turbine as the tide falls again, to generate electricity.

The Bay is also a paradise for marine life. The swift tidal currents create conditions perfect for the growth of teeming sea life. Large numbers of fish, whales and seabirds thrive there. Fishermen follow the Bay's rhythm for their catch. Some of the tide's power can be seen at the head of the Bay, where it has created large mud flats — home to thousands of migrating birds.

The tides look muddy because they eat away so much land as they surge in and out. The racing sea waters carved the Hopewell Cape Rocks into fantasy shapes. One day these rocks will fall — bit by bit, the tides are wearing them away. At low tide visitors can walk around the rocks, but must keep track of the time to avoid getting trapped by high tide. In the Bay of Fundy, it's no joke.

This Sausage Sizzles!

Not an illusion, not sleight of hand — the longest sausage in the world really went the distance.

The world's longest continuous sausage on record was an amazing 46.3 kilometres long. M&M Meat Shops partnered with J. M. Schneider to make the incredible sausage in Kitchener, Ontario, on April 28-29, 1995. It contained pork, water, milk ingredients, salt, toasted wheat crumbs, modified starch, spices, sodium and sodium nitrite (a preservative). Meat experts laboured for two days to make the gigantic sausage containing 315,000 sausage links in a continuous line. Then the record-breaker was cut up into portions and sold. Fifty cents from the price of each was donated to charity.

How Sweet It Is!

One of the sweetest delights in the world is tree sap, boiled down to concentrate its flavour. Sound ridiculous? Not if you've tasted maple syrup. Canada's First Peoples were tapping maple trees before Europeans came to Canada. Settlers caught on quickly. So it's no surprise that we find a way to celebrate our delicious syrup with a giant festival.

The Elmira Maple Syrup Festival is the biggest one in the world, with attendance topping 80,000.

The festival first took place in 1965. The Elmira Board of Trade and local townsfolk organized pancake meals topped with pure maple syrup. They held pancake-flipping contests, exhibitions of local arts and crafts, and a heritage display and tour. They expected 2,500 visitors that first year — and 10,000 people came. Later, to help serve the vast crowds, the town commissioned the world's biggest maple syrup bucket. The gigantic bucket holds a whopping 605 litres.

Each year the festival gets bigger, and the money it makes is put back into the community. Since it started, over $850,000 has been raised for the Elmira Region.

Humongous Cheese

In September of 1995 the world's biggest cheese was created. It weighed a whopping 26,900 kilograms, in one gigantic chunk. An eighteen-wheel refrigerated truck was adapted to store the cheese and transport it, and a viewing window was added.

But why make a piece of cheese so big? The Loblaws grocery chain wanted to call attention to the excellent nutritional value, taste and quality of Canadian cheese, so it asked cheese manufacturer Agropur of Granby, Quebec, to make the world's biggest cheese.

Simply creating the cheese took so much labour and resources that it boggles the mind. Agropur processed 245 tonnes of milk to create the huge hunk of cheddar. Ingredients had to be kept scrupulously clean and at stable temperatures, or the cheese would spoil.

The big cheese toured twenty Loblaws and Supercentre stores in Ontario and Quebec. After the tour, the cheese was cut into 18-kilogram blocks. It was still edible, still a good cheddar. It was sold, and some of the money raised from the sales was donated to children's hospitals.

So remember, if someone claims to be the big cheese in your town, correct them. There *was* a bigger one.

Way Long Bridge

Crossing it feels endless. Below it runs the sea, and huge waves strike the support pillars, save in the deep of winter when ice covers the Northumberland Strait.

The world's longest bridge over ice-covered waters opened on May 31, 1997, to join Prince Edward Island to New Brunswick. Confederation Bridge is 12.9 kilometres long and 11 metres wide, and it takes about ten minutes for a car to cross it. People aren't allowed to cross on foot or by bicycle — it would be too dangerous, due to high winds and narrow lanes. Pedestrians and cyclists get a free shuttle ride, though they might have to wait up to two hours for the lift.

The Confederation Bridge connects Borden-Carleton, P.E.I, and Cape Jourimain, N.B., across the narrowest part of the Northumberland Strait. It cost $1 billion to build, with the federal government helping to finance the costs. It took 5,000 workers, starting in 1993 and ending in 1997, to construct it. First the piers, pier shafts, main girders, drop-in girders and concrete box girders were precast in Bayfield, New Brunswick. The box girders connect the piers at the bottom for maximum strength — this is called post-tensioning — and ties the small parts together into one continuous structure. The precast pieces were shipped by land or water to the bridge site. Huge cranes put together the approach bridges — 1,300 metres in New Brunswick and 580 metres in P.E.I. Foundations were set on bedrock all across the strait. Then the Svanen, a unique giant floating crane, was used to place and join the main bridge parts.

At its highest point the bridge reaches 60 metres above the water, high enough to allow ships to pass beneath. There are ice shields on the piers to force the ice to travel up a cone shape, where it will crumble.

In case of problems, there are emergency phones and fire extinguishers every 750 metres, and a twenty-four-hour bridge patrol. The bridge has a hollow core housing cables and electrical services. Seventeen closed-circuit cameras keep all sections of the bridge in the sights of the operators, and 310 streetlights keep it lit. There are thirty-four traffic signals, normally all green. There's only one lane in each direction, so stopping on the bridge is forbidden. Concrete barriers that double as windbreaks run the entire length of the bridge, high enough that drivers can't see over the edge to the water below. The road surface is built of a specially treated long-lasting asphalt-cement mix, which minimizes spray in wet weather. There are 7,300 drain ports to keep the road clear. The bridge is expected to last a hundred years. It is curved because experts say accidents happen more on straight bridges.

In the old days P.E.I.'s mail was brought across the strait by canoe or ice boat. There was treacherous open water to cross, and rough ice in the winter, so the boats would often have to be carried. The island province is less isolated now. Bridge users say it beats waiting for the ferry — the usual way to make the crossing before Confederation Bridge existed.

Do more people go to P.E.I. now that the bridge is in place? Surveys say yes. P.E.I. had almost 1.2 million visitors in 1997, compared to 741,000 in 1996, before the bridge was completed. Even more people visited in 1998, bringing over $288 million to the island. Many people come just to experience crossing Confederation Bridge.

A Legendary Life-Saving Hero

"Doctors must go to the wounded, and the earlier the better," said Dr. Norman Bethune. The time was 1936. The place was Spain. The challenge was to save the lives of soldiers wounded while fighting a revolution. To do that, blood transfusions had to be given near where the fighting was actually happening. No one had ever brought those kinds of medical services to the brink of the battlefield before, but for Bethune, it was the obvious way to save lives. He bought a station wagon and created the world's first mobile blood-transfusion unit. He installed a refrigerator in the station wagon, and added sterilizing units and other medical equipment. He arranged for blood to be collected. Then, boldly, he and his team drove to the front lines, and began treating the wounded there.

Bethune set new standards for the treatment of soldiers. Today this kind of work, right in the field of combat, is expected, but in Bethune's time it was a radical new idea.

Bethune was also able to see the social problems behind health problems. If his patients became ill because of poverty and unhealthy conditions in crowded tenements, for example, he spoke out for change. Although it was almost unheard of, he created a health clinic for unemployed people in Montreal. He lobbied for reforms in health care. When he was young he had survived tuber-culosis — maybe that was why he never stopped seeing the world from the patient's point of view.

When the communist revolution in China attracted Bethune's

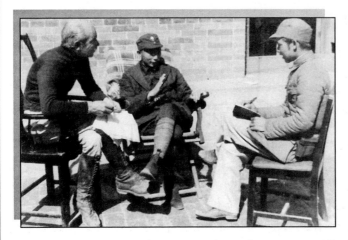

attention in 1938, the outspoken doctor travelled to the bloodiest battlefields to give medical aid to the soldiers. There he trained medics and doctors in the field. He formed the world's first mobile medical unit, carried on two mules. In spite of a shortage of money, antibiotics and surgical instruments, he saved countless lives. He went without sleep and food when the soldiers did. When he ran out of gloves to protect himself while he operated, he operated anyway. Bethune's dedication killed him. During an operation, he cut himself and developed an infection. He died in the hills of northern China.

Millions of Chinese revere Bethune as a legendary hero, a man of the people who cared so much for the wounded that he would not spare himself. They call him *Pai-ch'iu-en,* which means "White Seeks Grace." By his tomb at Shih-chia Chuang, in northern China, stand a larger-than-life statue, a pavilion, a museum and the Norman Bethune International Peace Hospital, all dedicated to him.

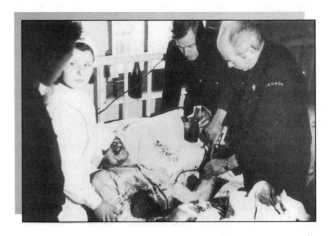

High-Tech Device Revolutionizes Blood Analysis

Astronauts use it. Paramedics in ambulances use it. Those caring for hand-sized babies in hospitals use it. It's even been used on the International Space Station. It's the i-Stat blood analyzing system, invented by Dr. Imants R. Lauks and his team at i-Stat Canada Limited. The i-Stat hit the North American market in 1992, after six years in development. For the first time ever, a hand-held device could swiftly deliver twelve common blood tests. The i-Stat is as accurate as standard laboratory tests, with a lot less work — plus there's no need to send the blood to a lab and wait for results to come back. The i-Stat uses only a few drops of blood, so tiny babies who are sick and might need many blood tests need fewer transfusions when the device is used.

How can such a small unit do all this? The i-Stat system uses solid-state electronics — miniature chips that have no moving parts — to analyze the blood. The drops of blood react with parts of the chips specially designed to "recognize" particular aspects of the blood's chemistry. So instead of technicians performing the tests, they are done by the machine right away. Results come up on a display screen. The i-Stat can even "talk" to other machines in hospitals or clinics.

Saving time in blood analysis can mean saving lives. The unit makes it possible to check on the condition of patients during surgery, at the site of an accident, and in places a doctor and a lab can't easily go — like outer space.

Beating the Sugar Disease

The invention of insulin could have made Frederick Banting millions of dollars. Instead, he gave rights to the patent to the University of Toronto, and from there to the Medical Research Council of Canada. Why?

Banting's childhood friend Jane died at the age of fourteen from diabetes. As he helped carry her coffin, he wondered why no doctor had found a cure for this terrible disease. He was appalled at her suffering and death.

By late October of 1920 Banting had become a young doctor practising in London, Ontario. He read a medical article by Moses Barron that got him thinking about diabetes. That night Banting awoke from sleep and wrote a note to himself so he wouldn't forget his idea. The reminder was this: to attempt research with dogs, tying off their pancreatic ducts to try to isolate and investigate the special chemicals the pancreas makes. This idea eventually led to the discovery of insulin, a treatment that allows 15 million diabetics around the world to live longer, healthier lives.

People with diabetes cannot properly digest and regulate sugars. The only treatment in 1920 was a restricted diet. Children and adult diabetics withered away and died, while their families and doctors watched helplessly. Banting had seen this for himself.

Once he had his idea, Banting needed a laboratory, an assistant and funds to support research. Dr. John Macleod of the University of Toronto first refused him, but Banting wouldn't give up. Macleod finally allowed him use of a lab during Macleod's summer vacation, plus the assistance of Charles Best, a graduate student. Demanding and frustrating research followed. When Banting and Best succeeded in restoring vigour to a diabetic dog by using their extract, Macleod was convinced. He brought in J.B. Collip, a skilled biochemist. Collip worked to refine and purify insulin so it could be safely given to people. Months of setbacks were finally followed by success.

Leonard Thompson, a fourteen-year-old who was dying of diabetes and who weighed only 30 kilograms, became the team's first patient. After Collip's injection the boy became alert, sat up and felt well. But how could enough insulin be produced to keep him and thousands of diabetics, who would need injections every day, well? How could the right dosages be calculated for different patients? How could a consistent strength of insulin be assured, when large-scale production began? Any differences between batches could mean death for the diabetics taking the insulin. There was no easy answer to all these questions. More research followed, by Collip and other scientists at the Connaught Laboratories.

Persistence paid off at last. Connaught Labs established the world standard for insulin — high quality and a consistent concentration. Dosages were worked out. Once the Connaught could supply enough insulin, many more patients were treated. Some famous ones included inventor Thomas Edison, writer and broadcaster H.G. Wells and King George V of England.

In 1923 Banting and Macleod shared the Nobel Prize for Medicine. Shocked that Best had been left out, Banting gave Best half his prize money. Macleod later shared his with Collip. Banting used his own share to fund the Banting Medical Research Foundation.

"I was not a brilliant student," Banting said, "but I had boundless curiosity and I worked very hard." He never imagined that he would be the person to help discover a way to save the lives of diabetics.

Canadian Connection Helps Conquer Polio

Most summers before 1954 brought not just warm weather, but a polio epidemic. Thousands of children were killed or paralyzed by the polio virus. Dr. Jonas Salk, an American microbiologist, developed a successful polio vaccine. A massive trial in 1954 in the United States, Canada and Finland showed it was effective and safe. Salk became famous overnight.

But no one knew the Canadian connection that made Salk's vaccine safe for *people*. All the polio viruses used during that trial were grown in a substance called Medium 199 in Toronto's Connaught Medical Research Laboratories. Then containers of the virus-loaded medium were shipped to the United States by car. If any accident disturbed the containers before the viruses reached the trial, the drivers had orders to pour gasoline on the cars and burn them!

Medium 199 was invented by Nova Scotia-born Raymond Crandall Parker, then doing research at Connaught Labs in Ontario. Before Medium 199, scientists grew their cultures in animal fluids. Salk had been growing polio virus from monkeys in a horse serum medium. His vaccine for polio could not be given to people, because the animal fluids would cause dangerous reactions. In 1953 Salk received a sample of Parker's Medium 199. He knew exactly what was in the nutrient broth — 60 ingredients including salts, vitamins, hormones and carbohydrates. He realized Medium 199 was safe for injecting into people. In fact, he was so sure of Parker's broth that within a day of getting it, he injected the first vaccine produced in it into his wife, his three sons and several hundred school children in Pittsburgh.

Years of research and trials, beginning just after World War II, had gone into the development of Medium 199. Parker's work gave Salk the means to stop the deadly polio epidemic, and other scientists the chance to do important research. Like many scientists, he is an unknown hero, without whom many lives could not have been saved.

Pacemaker Saves Thousands

It works twenty-four hours a day without you giving it a thought. The hardest working muscular organ in the body, it never rests — *flub-dub, flub-dub,* like clockwork. That rhythm is hard-wired into the nerves of your heart. If your heart beats too quickly or too slowly, not enough blood will get to important organs, like your brain. You'll keel over and might even black out. If your heart stops, you'll die.

In some people the heart's usual beating rhythm goes wrong. That's when the pacemaker makes a normal life possible. The pacemaker sends a very tiny electrical jolt to the heart regularly, so a normal heart rate is restored and maintained.

The pacemaker wasn't invented by a medical doctor, but by electrical engineer Dr. John Hopps of Canada's National Research Council (NRC) in Ottawa. Hopps first noticed that electricity could make a heart beat while working with Dr. Wilfred Bigelow at the Banting Institute in Toronto. In reviving animals that were victims of extreme cold, the scientists discovered that electrical impulses could restore a regular heartbeat, replacing the heart's own failed signal systems.

When Hopps was at the NRC in the early 1950s, he and his team built the first external pacemakers. Then NRC asked Smith and Stone Ltd. to manufacture them. Once a pacemaker was in the marketplace, it sparked interest and in turn stimulated research into smaller models, using the NRC's design principles. Doctors realized the potential of the pacemaker, and the race was on to develop one small enough to place inside the human chest cavity. The first pacemaker was implanted in a patient in 1958.

The insertion of a pacemaker makes a full life possible for thousands of people with heart problems. Today it is considered an almost routine operation. Routine, perhaps, but lifesaving and life-changing. Doctors Hopps and Bigelow have both received awards for their development of the pacemaker.

When Babies Are in Danger

The fire alarm sounds! For hospital workers this is a nightmare. How will they get all their patients to safety in time? Elevators stop running for safety reasons. Evacuation has to be done by the stairwells, with hospital staff carrying every patient. The nurses caring for newborn or sick babies are in real trouble. There are so many babies to carry out, and so few nurses. If they carry one or two babies at a time, they will never make it . . .

Too often in the past, nurses faced this crisis. Now hospital staff can grab the WEEVAC and tuck their tiny patients into secure pockets, six to a stretcher. Efficiently and safely, they can carry all the babies to safety. All because of Wendy Murphy, inventor of the world's only emergency evacuation stretcher for babies. The WEE-VAC will even help keep them warm — an urgent need for newborns.

Murphy didn't intend to become a famous inventor with her own company. But when she saw a problem she wanted to solve it. In 1987 a fire broke out in the Hospital for Sick Children in Toronto. At that time Murphy was working in the Neonatal Intensive Care Unit (ICU). Although the fire was located three floors below, smoke reached the ICU unit where she was working. The newborn babies in this unit could be quickly harmed by smoke, so the nurses had to move fast. How would they move the babies quickly, with perfect safety? They planned to rush their patients down the hall to another wing of the hospital, one that was unaffected by the fire. Firefighters were able to put out the fire and contain the smoke before evacuation was necessary. But what if they *hadn't* been able to do so?

The next morning, as hospital workers reviewed the crisis, they knew they needed a way to carry many babies down the stairs in safety. Nothing existed that could help them do that. Murphy had an idea. Two years earlier she had watched a television program showing Mexican babies being evacuated following a terrible earthquake, one infant to a stretcher. Murphy imagined a special stretcher with pockets and adjustable straps, which could evacuate six babies at once, in warmth and complete safety. Dr. Barry Smith asked Murphy to present her idea to the evacuation committee, with a drawing and a stretcher to demonstrate. After the meeting, Dr. Smith ordered ten of her stretchers at once, and encouraged her to make the units herself.

That's how WEEVAC-6, the six-infant emergency evacuation stretcher, was first produced. Murphy faced many challenges in designing and financing the production of her unique, award-winning stretchers. A special Mylar-laminated vinyl fabric in the pockets helps retain the babies' body heat, and the straps have Velcro to allow for different baby sizes. Hospitals around the world have bought them.

Murphy was asked to design stretchers for evacuating the elderly, too, and a cover to keep babies in a transport incubator safe from the cold. She has designed stretchers for compact storage and to get injured people out of tight situations. Her products now help in search and rescue, the Canadian Coast Guard, and emergency situations from Hawaii to New Zealand. "Inventors," Murphy says, "are adults who have kept their childlike wonder of the universe, still ask questions, and believe that their dreams are possible."

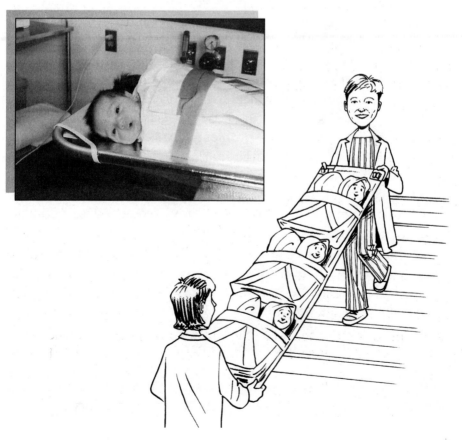

Dr. Murray's Miracle

The scene is an operating room in the early 1900s. The surgeon sews up the blood vessels and removes the clamps. Blood flows in the injured veins. An arm or leg has just been successfully repaired. Everything looks good. But a few hours or days later, the patient is in terrible pain, and in seconds is dead. A blood clot, formed at the site of the operation, has travelled to the brain or the heart. The operation succeeds, but the patient dies. In another scenario a blood clot may have blocked circulation to a patient's hand. The repaired limb has died and gangrene has set in. The hand has become poisonous, and must be amputated to save the patient's life . . .

Before a drug created by Dr. Gordon Murray, such stories were far too common.

Heparin, a drug made from dog liver, was discovered at Johns Hopkins University by Americans Jay McLean and William Howell. But McLean and Howell could not produce a drug safe for use in human beings.

Enter the Canadians. By 1928 insulin co-inventor Dr. Charles Best was the new head of the University of Toronto's Physiology Department, and an Associate Director of Connaught Laboratories, which produced insulin for the treatment of diabetes. Best recognized heparin's potential, and decided to solve the remaining problems with it — to purify the drug, produce it in quantity, and see if it could solve blood-clotting problems in human patients. The researchers included Dr. Arthur F. Charles, a chemist, and Dr. David A. Scott, who had helped with insulin production, but they needed a gifted surgeon, someone who could try out the drug during surgery on test animals. Dr. Gordon Murray, renowned surgeon at Toronto General Hospital, was invited to join the team.

For three years, 1933 to 1936, Charles and Scott purified and standardized heparin. But would it work? Dr. Murray conducted successful trials on animals, and then began to use heparin to save lives and limbs in his patients. By 1937 the drug had proven itself. At last Murray could safely perform surgery involving blood vessels and major organs, because using heparin made such operations safer.

Here's how it works: heparin acts by preventing blood from clotting too much — coagulating — at the site of an injury or operation. In medical terms it is an "anticoagulant." Murray kept blood vessels open and prevented blood clots from forming after surgery by injecting heparin into his patients. They healed and survived.

Murray lectured and wrote on the safe use of heparin, publishing his first paper on the subject in 1936. He created guidelines for dosages, since getting just the right dose was crucial. Too little heparin and a clot could form; too much and there could be excessive bleeding. In early trials by other doctors, patients actually bled to death. Gradually, heparin was accepted throughout North America, and then elsewhere, until its use became commonplace. The drug revolutionized surgery and saved millions of lives. It also paved the way for revolutionary surgical techniques such as organ transplants and open-heart surgery.

Murray and Best's team at Connaught had changed the face of medicine. Other anticoagulant drugs are available today, but heparin started it all.

A brilliant innovator and surgeon, Dr. Murray pioneered blood-vessel surgery. He performed the first heart surgery on a "blue baby" (so-called because of the colour caused by lack of oxygen in the blood), and the first kidney transplant in Toronto. In 1955 he was the first surgeon in the world to successfully transplant a human heart valve, giving many years of additional life to his patient. Where Murray led, the world followed.

Dr. Mak and Cell Suicide

Every cell in our bodies gets signals all the time. One of the most fascinating is the signal to commit suicide. When our bodies don't need a cell, it is told to kill itself. Sometimes that signal comes from inside the cell, sometimes from other cells. Cell suicide is called *apoptosis*. There's a "suicide bag" in most cells, a packet of enzymes that, if set free, destroys the cell. And that's just fine. Cell death is as important to good health as cell life, because some cells aren't supposed to live forever. They die and get replaced by new ones.

Cancer cells are cells that won't die when they should, and scientists have been trying to discover why for a long time. Called by some scientists "zombie" cells, because they can't be killed, these cells multiply, making more zombie cells, and creating tumours.

In 1998 scientists led by Dr. Tak Mak at the Ontario Cancer Institute/ Princess Margaret Hospital — one of the top cancer research and treatment centres in the world — discovered that the gene PTEN, isolated the year before by an American scientist, is actually the gene that can control the "zombie" phenomenon. In more scientific language, PTEN is a tumour-suppressor gene. Healthy cells have two PTEN genes. If a cell is missing one PTEN gene, or has a mutated PTEN, then another group of genes in the cell, sometimes called the survival pathway, gets turned on. That means that the message, "Live, live on, don't die," is sent all the time. This is very dangerous, because even if the cell is told to die, it hears the "live" message too. Given conflicting messages, the cell chooses to live. The cell has become a zombie cell — a cell that just won't die, no matter what. If that cell divides, making more zombies, then a cancerous tumour can result. Not only that, tumours without normal PTEN genes are much harder to kill. About 90 percent of chemotherapy drugs won't work on them. Knowing that, doctors can fine-tune treatment to use drugs that *will* work.

In those cancers without healthy PTEN genes (not *all* cancers lack them), it's as if the "off" switch is gone. Dr. Mak and his colleagues are determined to find a way to replace lost or damaged PTEN with healthy PTEN, or at least its enzyme. This would restore the cell's normal suicide pathway. As strange as it sounds, this would be a very good thing. Then, perhaps, the tumour cells would kill themselves, the way they are supposed to. This solution would use the body's *own* protective measures to help kill cancerous cells — a natural and healthy treatment.

Dr. Mak and Dr. Vuk Stambolic researched PTEN by breeding mice — called "knockout" mice — that were missing one healthy PTEN gene. These mice had a much higher tendency to develop certain kinds of tumours. Mice missing both copies of healthy PTEN died before birth.

Survivors of Mega-Chill

About 2 A.M. on February 23, 1994, two-year-old Karlee Kosolofski woke up, grabbed a jacket and boots and followed her father outside. No one saw her go. Robert Kosolofski went to work, unaware that his daughter was now locked out by the spring-loaded door. Karlee's mother Karrie slept on, unaware. Their home in Rouleau, Saskatchewan, was in the grip of the cold prairie winter. The temperature was -22.2°C. The child froze within twenty minutes, and wasn't found by her mother until 8 A.M. She was almost frozen solid by then.

Karlee's distraught mother could have given up hope, but she didn't. She called an ambulance. Paramedics rushed Karlee to hospital in Saskatoon. When they arrived, the little girl was clinically dead. Her core body temperature had fallen to 14.2°Celsius — an astounding difference of almost 23 degrees below normal body temperature of 37°C.

A team of doctors used a heart-lung machine to slowly warm Karlee over a period of five hours, and revive her. Remarkably, she had no brain damage. Her frostbitten left leg had to be amputated above the knee, and bone surgeries and skin grafts were needed, but the spunky toddler completely recovered in all other ways. Doctors were astonished. Many called her recovery a miracle. Today Karlee is a spirited nine-year-old who does what many other children of her age do. She plays with her friends, loves to swim, and has even taken dance classes.

Extreme cold slows down metabolism, stops the heart and puts a person into a deep coma. Ironically, it is the deep cold that saved Karlee's brain from damage, because it slows down the brain's need for oxygen and nutrients. Scientists are learning more and more about reviving people from hypothermia, but the victims must be found in time, and treated quickly, in exactly the right ways.

Karlee's case is extraordinary. No one before her had ever registered a body temperature so cold, and still recovered.

A strange twist of fate helped to save another child in similar circumstances years later. On February 24, 2001, thirteen-month-old Erika Nordby slipped out of bed in Edmonton, Alberta, and crawled outside. At 3 A.M. her mother awakened and began a frantic search for her. Erika was found in the back yard, frozen stiff. The temperature was -20°C. Emergency medical technicians Tammy Hills and Jason Visscher were the first to arrive on the scene, at 3:49 A.M. Soon after, ambulance paramedics arrived. One of them was Krista Rempel, who had helped to first treat and then transport Karlee Kosolofski. She knew there was hope for Erika, and was part of the team working to save the baby's life.

A breathing tube could not be inserted down Erika's throat at first, because her mouth was frozen shut. But she was given advanced CPR and warm IV fluids and rushed to the University of Alberta Hospital. There, like Karlee, she was found to be clinically dead — she wasn't breathing, she had no heartbeat, and her core temperature had dropped to 16°C. Her heart started again in hospital, and five and a half hours later her body temperature had returned to normal. Five weeks later Erika went home, having required only a few small skin grafts.

Terry Fox Continues to Inspire Us

A young man with an artificial leg running across Canada — it is an image we will never forget.

When Terry Fox of Port Coquitlam, British Columbia, was only eighteen, he lost most of his right leg to bone cancer. The night before the operation he dreamed of running a marathon to raise awareness of cancer, plus money for research. Moved by the suffering he saw among other cancer patients, he vowed to help bring a cure for this terrible disease closer. The day after his dream, his leg was amputated 15 centimetres above the knee.

Three years later Fox was ready. Starting at St. John's, Newfoundland, he began to run across Canada on his artificial leg. He called his journey the Marathon of Hope. Always athletic, he ran an incredible marathon of 43 kilometres every day, seven days a week. From April 12, 1980, to the end of August, ignoring his own pain, Fox awed spectators as he ran on, his gait adapted to swing his artificial leg forward. He had covered 5,376 kilometres when a recurrence of the cancer forced him to stop running, just outside Thunder Bay, Ontario, on September 1. A stunned nation mourned as Terry Fox grew worse. He died eleven months later, on June 28, 1981.

That first marathon raised almost $25 million for cancer research. And a promise was made to Fox that annual runs to raise money for cancer research would continue. The Terry Fox Foundation, headed by his brother Darrell, keeps the promise. The Foundation organizes annual runs in 55 countries around the world, and distributes the money raised to institutions accredited by the International Union Against Cancer, in Geneva, Switzerland.

Terry Fox so moved us by his example of courage, perseverance and unselfishness that marathons run in his name continue to grow. They have raised about $270 million worldwide for cancer research. Abier Lahan, one of the organizers in Syria, says that the marathon there helps individuals realize that they can make a difference.

Today, Terry Fox continues to inspire millions of people the world over. Steve Fonyo, with an artificial limb on his left leg, completed Fox's route in his cross-Canada Journey for Lives in 1983-1985.

As Terry said in 1980, "I just wish people would realize that anything's possible if they try, that dreams are made if people try."

The World's Longest Wheelchair Journey

Rick Hansen's Man in Motion Tour around the world in 1985-87 set a record as the world's longest wheelchair journey. It was a unique journey, by a unique man.

As a boy, Rick Hansen loved sports and fishing. Coming home from a fishing trip in 1973, he hitched a ride in the back of a pick-up truck. The truck crashed and Hansen, then just fifteen, was left a paraplegic. Because his legs were paralyzed, he faced spending his life in a wheelchair.

Hansen's life had changed forever, but he didn't give up his dreams. While in rehabilitation in a hospital, he began to set goals. He was determined to continue his education. After high school he graduated in physical education from the University of British Columbia, the first student with a physical disability to do so. His love of sports continued. He became a champion wheelchair athlete, winning three world championship wheelchair marathons and competing in the 1984 Paralympics. But Hansen had even bigger dreams. He wanted to create awareness of the potential that people with disabilities had. He wanted to inspire people to believe in their dreams. And most of all, he wanted to make a difference.

Rick Hansen decided a journey would attract attention and raise awareness. He would donate the funds raised to spinal-cord injury research. He embarked on an incredible quest: to wheel himself around the world. It was a marathon to beat all other marathons, never done before or since. Many said it was impossible. But Hansen didn't believe them.

With a small group of friends he began his journey on March 21, 1985. For more than two years he travelled through thirty-four countries — over rugged mountain ranges and through punishing desert heat, frigid winter blasts and torrential rains. He wore out 94 pairs of gloves and 160 wheelchair tires on his journey. It took him an average of eight hours and 9,000 strokes a day to travel 80 to 112 kilometres. In all, he wheeled 40,074 kilometres — the full circumference of the earth — using the muscle power of his arms and the determination in his heart. His 792 days on the road raised donations of $20 million to support spinal-cord injury research, rehabilitation and prevention, as well as wheelchair sports. Hansen finished his remarkable feat on May 22, 1987.

With the money he raised, Hansen established the Man in Motion Legacy Fund, which continues to contribute millions of dollars to spinal-cord injury research. Today, as President and CEO of the Rick Hansen Institute at the University of British Columbia, he continues to work toward a more rapid discovery of a cure for spinal injuries. The field of spinal-cord injury is richer by more than $100 million because of his efforts. About 90 percent of the knowledge in spinal-cord research has been learned in the last ten years.

Says Hansen, "If you believe in a dream and have the courage to try, great things can be accomplished."

On September 26, 2002, Jeff Adams showed that even the Everest of staircases can't stop a determined wheelchair athlete. He set a world record: the first person to hand power a wheelchair up the CN Tower's 1,760 steps.

To kick off an awareness campaign called Step Up to Change, Adams climbed the stairs in five and a half hours, powered only by his muscles. It was a gruelling feat, equal to climbing a 113-storey building. He trained for an entire year to prepare for the climb. Using a specially designed light wheelchair that could roll backwards only, Adams pulled himself up with one arm on the hand railing, and boosted himself with a crutch under his other arm.

Why did thirty-one-year-old Adams, an athlete with five medals from the Paralympic Games in Sydney, plus six world records, make the climb? In his own words, because "stairs are one of the most obvious, and visual, of the many barriers to access" that persons with disabilities encounter. He wants to educate people about the importance of making a "barrier-free" society that includes everyone. Step Up to Change focuses on students across Canada — those who will make tomorrow's laws and construct tomorrow's buildings — so that they will learn to appreciate the abilities of all members of society, including those with disabilities.

A busy motivational speaker and athlete, Adams took time off from the international sports circuit to make the climb. Funds for the educational program are handled by the Canadian Foundation for Physically Disabled Persons.

Dojo Demolition

It looked like a movie set. It seemed like special effects. But it was real. Karate alone was used to completely flatten a large home in Canada, in just over three hours. The astounding feat was performed by fifteen people, using their bare hands and feet.

We've all seen it done with heavy machinery — an old house reduced to piles of rubble. The job is expensive and loud. Diesel engines power a front-end loader or a wrecking crane, and the work generally takes hours. Before heavy machinery existed, large axes and hammers were used to do the job. When properly trained, the human hand or foot can be as powerful as any of these tools. And fast, too. A single karate dojo (a gym where sports such as judo and karate are performed) set out to prove this.

On May 11, 1996, a ten-room home in Saskatchewan was demolished without the use of a single tool. Fifteen members of the Aurora Karate Dojo did the job by hand and foot in 3 hours, 6 minutes and 50 seconds — the fastest human demolition of a house ever recorded.

World Record Swimmer

Would you volunteer to swim for more than twenty hours in brutal conditions? What if there were lampreys in the water with you, and you got bitten? What if there were oil spills to clog your nose and mouth, waves hitting you in the face, and winds to blow you off course? Would you keep going?

Marilyn Bell did. When she was only sixteen the Toronto-born teenager became the first swimmer to conquer Lake Ontario, crossing it in less than twenty-two hours. It was a remarkable, record-setting feat that made Bell famous. She endured when other swimmers withdrew, beaten by the frigid, rough lake. And she hadn't even planned to make the swim at first.

The Canadian National Exhibition (CNE) in Toronto had offered thirty-four-year-old American swimmer Florence Chadwick $10,000 to complete the swim across the lake. She was a famed long-distance swimmer, widely believed to be the best in the world. Relatively unknown Marilyn Bell, and another Canadian, twenty-eight-year-old Winnie Roach, entered the race for the sake of Canadian pride.

Bell expected to lose the race honourably — not even *she* knew her own strength. She hadn't learned to swim until the age of nine, and she had never been a fast swimmer. But her coach, Gus Ryder, saw greatness in her. He set up the swim for his young protégé, knowing she had a level of courage and stamina far greater than others'.

Around 11 P.M. on September 8, 1954, Chadwick, Roach and Bell entered Lake Ontario. They had chosen to swim from Youngstown, New York, at the mouth of the Niagara River, to the CNE grounds at Toronto's lakeside. Conditions were punishing. Estimates put the waves about 5 metres high. The water was a chilling 18.3°C. Eels attacked Bell's legs. Ryder, from a boat by her side, urged her on. As the night wore on and the lake took its toll, others in the boat argued that Bell should be pulled from the water, that she would drown. But she kept going.

After 20 kilometres Chadwick had to withdraw, suffering from stomach pains and vomiting. Though a strong distance swimmer, Roach, too, was forced to give up some time later, exhausted by the difficult conditions. Bell herself was driven far off course by strong winds and waves. She was on her way to a 64-kilometre swim to cover the 51.5-kilometre distance. Still Ryder shouted encouragement.

Bell alone stayed the distance. Swimming through her exhaustion, her absolute trust in Ryder kept her going. She reached the shore just west of the CNE, 21 hours and 59 minutes after entering the lake, at 8:15 P.M. on September 9. In Toronto the media had blanketed the city with hourly updates on the race. Thousands of people gathered to give Bell an emotional welcome — estimates of the crowd varied from 50,000 to 300,000 cheering fans. Today Bell cannot even remember the finish of the race. She was too exhausted.

The next year Marilyn Bell swam the English Channel on her second try, entering the record books as the youngest to conquer the Channel ever. It took her fourteen and a half hours. In 1956, again on her second try, she was praised as the first woman and the youngest athlete to swim the Straits of Juan de Fuca between Vancouver Island and the State of Washington. She swam the 30.5-kilometre strait in an astonishing ten and a half hours.

Though Marilyn Bell's feat earned her the title "First Lady of the Lake," she insisted she was an average person. Still celebrated today for her amazing sports achievements, she urged others to follow their dreams, to try again, even when they had failed. She should know. Two of her record-breaking swims were on second tries. For sheer guts, courage and determination, astonishing in an athlete so young, she's a Canadian icon.

First to Run the Great Wall of China

In 1982 David Adie, a Vancouver teacher, talked to a troubled youth about overcoming barriers. The two had the idea of running the Great Wall of China — the largest man-made barrier in the world. Adie promised to do it with the boy, to inspire other young people.

Over the next twelve years Adie left teaching to work as an acting and dance instructor, and never quite got around to fulfilling his promise. But when he heard that the boy had committed suicide, he was shocked into renewing his promise, this time to himself.

Adie's own challenge hit in 1990, when a rare disease of the nerves and muscles, Guillain-Barré Syndrome, paralyzed him. Doctors told him he might die, but Adie proved them wrong, even learning how to walk and talk again over the next year and a half. He had always liked to run, and had even trained for the Canadian Olympic team in 1980. Determination restored his abilities. In 1994, at age thirty-five, he arrived in China, ready to run the Great Wall. But the Chinese government wasn't ready for him — they claimed the run was impossible.

Adie's official start was on July 1 — Canada Day — but many obstacles stood in his way. Inaccurate maps led him astray seven times, once stranding him alone in the desert; he ran out of food and water; sandstorms nearly swept his camp away; he was chased by wild camels. But it got even worse. Adie ran out of funds when the Chinese government demanded a $20,000 permission fee up front. His Chinese support team quit. Sponsors (including the Canadian government) pulled out, assuming Adie would fail. His project co-ordinator resigned.

Finally Adie finished the run in secret with his brother — just the two of them. The run was an incredible combination of highs and lows. The brothers were arrested four times, and nearly shot. Adie experienced the awesome grandeur of running across mountains and through breathtaking gorges; he experienced sadness when he found and buried a dead girl. Villagers gave him aid. One old Chinese man fulfilled his lifetime's wish by thanking a Canadian for medical aid received long ago from a doctor trained by Dr. Norman Bethune.

Adie finished his run on October 7, 1994. He wore out seven pairs of sneakers, and covered over 5,000 kilometres in ninety-nine days. He arrived home in Canada with a new vision. He founded the "Yes I Can!" Children's Foundation International, and Steps 2 Peace, a series of events around the world to inspire children and promote world peace. He went on to run in Japan in 1995, Singapore and the Philippines in 1996-97, Great Britain and Ireland in 1997, and Australia in 1999 (to raise money for the Australian Teenage Cancer Patients Society). Then he went back to Australia to talk to young people across the continent.

What's it all for? Adie — who refused to be included in *The Guinness Book of Records* — says it's for the children. He is still living his promise.

Longest Water-Skiing Marathon

Water-skiing takes a lot of strength and stamina. On waves it takes more of both. Two Canadians decided to push the limit for charity. Ralph Hildebrand and Dave Phillips decided to try to ski around Indian Arm (a deep inlet north of Vancouver, British Columbia) and Rocky Point Park (at the south end of Vancouver Island), to raise money for cystic fibrosis sufferers. Their planned route covered a distance of over 2,000 kilometres. Some friends thought they had lost their minds, since that much skiing can be punishing to the human body. But they succeeded.

It was a remarkable feat of endurance. Phillips already held several records for water-skiing and for endurance snow skiing.

However, Hildebrand suffered temporary nerve damage during their ski marathon for charity; one of his legs swelled to twice its normal size. Despite the pain, he decided on the advice of a physician to continue, completed the course, and was able to walk the next day.

Hildebrand and Phillips water-skied for more than two days, ending on June 12, 1994. They covered an amazing 2,152.3 kilometres around Indian Arm, and were on the water for 56 hours, 35 minutes and 3 seconds. They raised more than $25,000 for sufferers of cystic fibrosis.

Yo, Eddie!

The fastest yo-yo trick performer in the world is Eddie McDonald, who can pack a sizzling thirty-five tricks into only 60 seconds. On July 22, 1999, at Toronto's Paulson Street Parkette, he set that record — the Most Yo-Yo Tricks in One Minute.

Can you Walk the Dog, or do the Sleeper, the Creeper, the Forward Pass, the Breakaway, the Man on the Flying Trapeze and the Elevator? Eddie McDonald started working on yo-yo tricks like these when he was just a kid. That was only the beginning. The Land of Yo, as yo-yo players and collectors sometimes call it, fascinated him. Soon he was practising for hours a day. Now people pay to watch him work his magic.

Fast Eddie doesn't lead the world just in record-swift yo-yo tricks. He also makes his living performing a large repertoire of tricks, and selling instruction booklets. He has performed live in fifteen countries around the world.

It wasn't easy to become this fast and this good with a yo-yo. Eddie McDonald got his first one when he was eleven years old, but took five years to master the basic tricks. He practised nearly every day, using an instruction booklet as his teacher. What is his hardest trick? He balances a quarter on a spectator's ear, and knocks it off with his yo-yo — without hurting the volunteer.

The Older the Better

The oldest person to ski to the North Pole is Jack Mackenzie of Stittsville, Quebec. In 1999 he covered the 100-kilometre trip from his base camp to the Pole, *at the age of 77*, in less than six days. Two explorers — Canadian Richard Weber and Russian Mikhail Malakhov — led a nine-member team, including Mackenzie, to the Pole. It's a dangerous journey, even for much younger men and women. No one as old as Mackenzie had ever made the trip by skis, but he is so fit that he could ski the gruelling landscape of the far north for five to seven hours every day during the expedition.

Adventure is in Mackenzie's blood. He was a pilot for the Royal Canadian Air Force during World War II, and has travelled to the seven continents of the world, including a 4,000-kilometre journey across China, a foray to the west coast of Greenland, and the crossing of the Drake Passage to Antarctica.

Jack Mackenzie — living proof that getting older doesn't mean slowing down.

Youngest Organ Transplant

When Sarah Marshall was 177 days old — not yet six months of age — she became the youngest patient in the world to receive multiple organ transplants. Sarah received a new stomach, bowel, liver and pancreas on August 7, 1997, at the London Health Sciences Centre (LHSC) in London, Ontario.

There were indications of problems even before Sarah's birth on Valentine's Day, 1997. Ultrasound images showed that she had an enlarged bladder. Doctors now suspect that her bladder interfered with the natural development of her intestines. Sarah threw up her first meal of breast milk, and was rushed to Toronto's Hospital for Sick Children for emergency surgery. She was one day old when surgeons cut open her abdomen and discovered she was in real trouble. Sarah had megacystis microcolon intestinal hypoperistalsis syndrome — a very rare condition.

Those long words mean that her bladder was much too big and

her colon much too small. The normal contractions of muscles in the intestines to help digest food weren't happening. Sarah also had a ruptured appendix and a twisted bowel. She began a long battle to survive — and proved to be a very strong fighter.

Despite many operations to help Sarah over the next five months, her liver failed and she began to bleed internally. Her only hope — and it was a slim hope — was a transplant of nearly *all* her abdominal organs. But they would have to come from a baby of her size and blood type, and time was running out.

Sarah had only hours left to live when a call came in from London. A family had lost their infant, but in an incredible act of generosity they were willing to let their child's organs be used as transplants to save another life. Sarah was rushed to LHSC and into surgery. Never before had so many transplants been attempted on such a young, tiny baby.

Nine hours later Sarah was wheeled out of the operating room, but she wasn't out of the woods yet. Drugs had to be given to prevent rejection of the organs, and still there were more emergencies over the next three months. Not until the end of November was she allowed to go home.

A party was held for Sarah at the LHSC in February, 1998, to call attention to the success of her transplants. Doctors pleaded with Canadians to consider donating organs, especially those of children, to help save lives.

Sarah is thriving — a testament to the world-class skills of her surgeons, the generosity of one special family, and her amazing will to live.

Not Too Small to Be Smart

Born January 1, 1994, she weighs just 3.6 kilograms and can respond to nearly one thousand hand signals and verbal commands. Never let it be said that a dog is too small to be smart! Chanda-Leah, a champagne-coloured toy poodle from Hamilton, Ontario, so impressed the publishers of *The Guinness Book of World Records* that they created a new category for her — World's Leader in Most Tricks

Performed by a Dog. Chanda's owner claims she can count, add, subtract and multiply numbers from one to ten; spell, rock a cradle and put her teddy bear into a buggy, cover it with a sheet and take it for a walk. She will fetch what she is asked for, not something else.

She recognizes hundreds of commands. She can untie three knots, bring a tissue to someone who has sneezed, open and close doors, walk on barrels and balls, bowl with a toy ball and pins and recognize mail with her name on it.

Owner Sharon Robinson is not a dog trainer. She noticed that Chanda enjoyed learning tricks and learned them quickly, so she kept teaching the little dog more and more. Sharon first suspected Chanda's intelligence when the dog rang a bell in her puppy cage to let her owner know it was time for a bathroom break.

Chanda has appeared on television shows, including *Live! With Regis and Kathy Lee* and *The Maury Povich Show*. Her talents might have led Chanda to an entertainment career, but that's not what Robinson wanted. Instead, Chanda visits schools, churches, nursing homes and hospitals, bringing laughter and amazement wherever she goes.

Sharon named Chanda after a chandelier because she seems to light up a room. The second part of her name, Leah, means "weak eyes." Chanda's eyes tear. But she can still recognize all the letters of the alphabet, the numbers from 1 to 100, and hundreds of hand signals. Some people think she is the world's smartest dog.

Occasionally, feats are accomplished by accident.

Hamlet the cat managed to escape from his cage in the cargo hold of an aircraft that had taken off from Toronto in January, 1984. A cargo hold is full of interesting places to hide, and Hamlet did just that. He hid so well that no one could find him at the next stop, or the next, or the next . . .

Hamlet eluded all attempts to rescue him — for *seven* weeks! When he was caught at last, in February of 1984, the Canadian stowaway had travelled a record 965,580 kilometres.

Peering into the Atom

You can't see them, but everything — your hand, the seat you're sitting on, this book — is made up of atoms. For nine years Canada gave a home and a top-notch workplace to the man who helped us understand atoms — Ernest Rutherford.

It takes special equipment to see things so small. At a time when few machines existed to see things that closely, Rutherford made sense of the unseen workings of the atom. In 1902, at only twenty-seven, Rutherford became Macdonald Professor of Physics at McGill University in Montreal. Born in Nelson, New Zealand, he had studied in England at first, but was not offered a professorship there. Attracted by the well-equipped facilities at McGill, he was glad to come to Canada to have use of the Macdonald Physics Building, then one of the best-equipped laboratories in the world. Frederick Soddy, who was later to win the Nobel Prize, assisted him.

Rutherford designed and performed very precise experiments at McGill, proving that atoms of radioactive matter, such as uranium, broke apart *all by themselves*. Once broken, they changed into something *different* — no longer the same material at all. These atoms went through a series of transformations, giving off rays of energy as they did. (For example, radioactive uranium eventually breaks down into lead via a process called radioactive decay.)

The idea that uranium could turn into lead *by itself* was so radical that the university at first asked Rutherford to delay publishing his work — such a provocative claim might do damage to McGill's reputation. But he and Soddy *did* publish, and their findings brought the study of atoms into a new era. Before Rutherford's experiments, the rays given off by matter like radioactive uranium had been a mystery. His work unravelled the secrets of radioactivity and the energy produced by atomic fission (the way energy is produced in the sun).

His reputation made, Rutherford was offered a position in Manchester, England. He went on to discover the nucleus of the atom. Considered today to be the greatest experimental physicist of the twentieth century, he won the 1908 Nobel Prize in Chemistry for his work.

Because of Rutherford's spectacular work at McGill, we understand the secrets of the atom much better. In his honour, the university named its physics laboratories after him.

Forgotten Woman Scientist Was Co-Discoverer of Radon

It's an important scientific achievement to discover a new element. A Canadian woman did so at a time when women were expected to stay at home and leave science to men. She was a bold and piercingly intelligent pioneer, who discovered a new radioactive element called radon in her work with Professor Ernest Rutherford.

While Rutherford was at McGill, Harriet Brooks became his first graduate student, his co-researcher and his lifelong friend. Rutherford gave Brooks the task of identifying the emanation given off by radium, the first radioactive element to be discovered. (France's Marie Curie had already discovered radium in 1898, isolating it from a rock called pitchblende.) Early in the 1900s, Brooks and her team discovered that the "emanation" was a new element, one eventually called radon. The discovery was an important part of the process of understanding radioactive decay. Brooks also described the ejection of particles during the radioactive process, later called the recoil theory. She worked at the Cavendish Lab in Cambridge, England, with J.J. Thomson, another pioneer in nuclear physics. Rutherford would later join Thomson at the Cavendish, and become head of the lab in his turn.

Rutherford was always careful to give Brooks the credit she deserved, but the rest of the academic community would not accept a woman as a serious physicist. Brooks's own papers were ignored, and her findings then "discovered" by other scientists. She eventually ceased active research, and died of radiation-related illnesses contracted during her work.

Born to a relatively poor family in Exeter, Ontario, Brooks was able to attend university only because her brilliance as a student won her scholarships. In an obituary published in the journal *Nature*, Rutherford said that "next to Madame Curie, Brooks was the most outstanding woman in the field of radioactivity." The article went on to say that he "credited her identification of emanation (radon) as a vital piece of work that had led him to propose the theory of the transmutation of one element into another. . . . A subsequent piece of her research . . . was a key step to disentangling the complexities of radioactive decay. Finally, there was the discovery of the recoil of the radioactive atom."

Brooks was the only physicist who worked with all three of the great nuclear physicists: Ernest Rutherford, J.J. Thomson and Marie Curie. All three were awarded Nobel Prizes for their work, to which Brooks had made invaluable contributions.

A New Way to Study Atoms

As scientists studied atoms through the years, they made more and more discoveries. But studying atoms in solid matter is especially difficult. The building blocks of the universe are too small to see by ordinary means.

Physicist Bertram Brockhouse worked at the Chalk River nuclear facility — Canada's first experimental nuclear reactor — in the 1950s. At Chalk River, scientists produced electricity using nuclear reactions, but they also researched atoms and the way they behave in solids. They sent beams of neutrons (very small particles with no electrical charge, which occur in the nucleus of most atoms) into matter. These neutrons were still invisible to the naked eye, but the path of the neutrons, after they had hit something and scattered, could be traced. And this told the scientists something about what the neutrons had hit. In effect, Brockhouse had invented a new method to peer into atoms, using this process called neutron scattering. As Brockhouse put it, "what we basically do in physics is push something and see what happens." He had used the neutrons to "push something" so he could see what happened, and shared the Nobel Prize in Physics in 1994 for his work.

The machine Brockhouse invented was the triple-axis spectrometer. He used it to investigate crystals, by putting a sample of a crystal into the machine. The spectrometer sent a beam of neutrons into a crystal at adjustable angles and intensities. Collisions with the crystal scattered the neutrons. Changes in the neutrons' speed told Brockhouse a lot about the vibrations between the atoms in the crystal. And *that* told him about the forces between atoms. Would these forces be the same in all kinds of crystals? Brockhouse tried different crystals to see what would happen. Different kinds of crystals produced different changes in the neutrons' speed.

Brockhouse may not have been able to see the atoms with his eyes, but his machine gave mathematical "pictures" of them. How? Brockhouse positioned a second crystal so the neutrons leaving the test crystal would pass through that too. The second crystal bent the neutron beams — how much they bent depended on the speed they were travelling — so he could then calculate how fast they were moving when they left the test crystal. Detecting their speed helped him "see" the forces between the atoms.

Today thousands of researchers use neutron scattering in many fields: chemistry, biology, engineering and materials physics — the study of how atoms behave in solid matter.

After Brockhouse's invention, scientists made many advances in understanding atoms. Upon receiving his Nobel Prize, Brockhouse said, "I was in the right place at the right time. We were intellectual explorers — we were like the first explorers to cross the Atlantic, finding out that it was not a narrow sea but a wide ocean."

A Black Hole Is Not a Hole

A black hole is not a hole — in fact, it's more like the opposite. Astronomers think that black holes are created when very old, very big stars collapse in on themselves. They believe that our galaxy revolves around an incredibly massive black hole at its centre, containing about 2.6 million times the amount of matter in Earth's sun. (In fact, most astronomers believe *every* galaxy has a black hole at its centre.) A black hole is the ultimate gravity well, a sort of gigantic vacuum cleaner sucking in anything that comes too close. At its centre, matter is crushed so densely that it disappears forever. Not even light can escape from a black hole. Inside one, the intense gravity slows down time and stretches out space — the very laws of the universe change.

Called "black" because they give off no light and cannot be seen directly, black holes are the phantoms of the universe. They can be detected only by their effects on nearby stars, comets, planets, gases and radio waves. How do you study something that can't be seen? By noticing everything *around* it; by understanding the usual behaviour of stars, and seeing puzzling exceptions. For example, if a planet changes its orbit where there is no other reason for it to change, perhaps a black hole is nearby, pulling it out of position.

At the centre of our galaxy, stars orbit about an invisible point at extraordinary speeds. What could keep them there, except a super-sized black hole, with its massive gravity? Without such a force, the stars should fly off in many directions. Strong emissions in the radio wavelengths from this invisible "point," called Sagit-

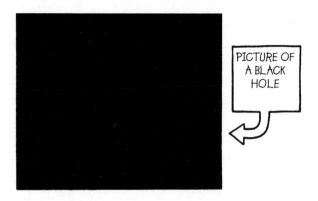

tarius A* (A-star), have also been detected. Enough odd behaviours like this, each agreeing mathematically with the others, might confirm the location of a black hole.

Do black holes sound complicated? Werner Israel thought not. Despite their huge size and many strange properties, Israel created a simple way to describe them using only their mass, spin and electrical charge. Of all other things in the universe, only elementary particles like electrons can be described in so simple and straightforward a way. Many awards have been given to Israel for his brilliant and elegant theory.

Werner Israel, a physicist and cosmologist, studied the stars, and the history and size of the universe. He was born in Germany, grew up in South Africa, studied in Ireland, then came to Canada and became an assistant professor at the University of Alberta in Edmonton in 1958. There he spent his working life, and in 1967 developed the first logically precise theory that dealt with the simplicity of black holes' essential features. It was an extremely elegant explanation for something very complex.

After nearly forty years in Edmonton, Israel is now Professor Emeritus of Physics at the University of Victoria.

A New View of the Milky Way

We live in the Milky Way galaxy. When we look in the night sky, away from strong lights, we see a bright band of stars. That's part of the Milky Way. We now know that the Milky Way is a spiral galaxy, but that is not obvious. To see it that way, you'd have to stand millions of light-years away and look at it from the top or bottom. Or you'd have to be a clever astronomer, like John Plaskett.

Plaskett didn't even become an astronomer until 1903, when he was forty years old. Before that he worked as a technician in the Physics Department of the University of Toronto, earning his degree at night. After years of careful work watching stars to track the movements of our own galaxy and to map its shape, he amazed the scientific world in 1930 by describing the Milky Way as clearly as if he stood far off in space. He even figured out that it was turning, and how long it took for it to turn around in space — an incredible 220 million years. With a colleague, Plaskett calculated that the centre of our galaxy is 33,000 light years away from Earth — an important breakthrough.

Plaskett worked at the Dominion Observatory in Ottawa, where he designed his own precision equipment. When he needed a larger telescope so he could see deeper into space, he talked the Canadian government into funding it. Then he designed much of it, and supervised its construction near Victoria, British Columbia. It was finished in 1918, becoming the world's largest telescope at that time.

Before his major discovery, Plaskett had begun the first systematic survey of twin stars, and became famous in 1922 when he discovered that what was thought to be a single star was, in fact, the heaviest then-known pair of stars — more than 100 times heavier than our Sun and more than 10,000 times brighter. The pair was named in his honour.

So important was Plaskett's work in the field of astronomy that a local asteroid in our solar system, and a crater on the moon, have also been named after him.

Exactly where is the centre of the Milky Way?

That bright spot in the centre of the lower third of the picture (above right) is the Sagittarius star cloud. The centre of the Milky Way is a bit to the right, behind a dark patch of dust-filled gas. So much dust hides our galaxy's centre that only a *tiny* fraction of one percent of its visible light reaches our eyes.

The brighter stars of Sagittarius form a "teapot" shape, with the Sagittarius star cloud looking like steam coming from the teapot's spout.

Photo taken by Glenn LeDrew with a 28-millimetre lens on a 35-millimetre camera and with Kodak P1600 slide film, from the Madawaska Highlands in eastern Ontario. Exposure was fifteen minutes, tracked on a motorized tracking mount.

Geologist Uncovered Secrets of the Earth

Dig up a layer of coal, and you'll find coal tree-roots and coal ferns. Why? Every bit of coal on Earth used to be part of a swamp or forest. The trees and plants rotted and got covered over by layers of rock. Pressure and eons of time transformed the plant life into coal. Today we accept this fact, but in the early 1800s no one knew that coal beds were the locations of ancient swamps and forests — until William Edmond Logan did his work.

In the 1830s Logan was the first to draw the layers of rock he traced near coal fields — cross-sections of the Earth's crust drawn like a vertical slice. It's like cutting through a many-layered cake, then drawing the layers neatly on a paper and labelling them — cake, jam, cake, cream, cake, icing . . . Of course, rock layers are a lot more complicated. Logan's technique would become a major tool in the study of geology.

Logan was born in Montreal, but he made his discovery in Wales. He saw huge fossil roots in the clay layers below seams of Welsh coal. This discovery proved that coal is formed from rotted vegetation. Logan verified his discovery in North America, too.

He is also remembered as head of the huge Geological Survey of The Province of Canada (the name given to the union of Upper and Lower Canada in 1840). The Survey was begun in 1842 and took more than two decades to complete. Logan discovered the fault zone between the old and rugged bedrock of the Canadian Shield and the younger Appalachian mountains in eastern Quebec. Now called Logan's Line, the fault is hundreds of kilometres long.

Logan was no armchair scientist, leaving the field work to his staff. He paddled the coast of the Gaspé peninsula with a guide, scrambled up mountains, collected rock samples and made geological maps. Painstaking and practical, he laid firm scholarly foundations for geology in Canada. His team's findings were published in an 1865 book, *The Geology of Canada*.

Logan was the first Canadian-born scientist ever invited to join the Royal Society of London, which was for many years the world's most prestigious association of learned men.

Canadian Pushes Field Dig for Peking Man

Ever wonder what your earliest ancestor looked like? Scientists called anthropologists have been studying that question for a long time. They search for the bones of ancient humans and put together a picture of those early human ancestors. For a long time anthropologists in Europe tried to find the earliest human. Then a sensational find made them look to China. Dr. Davidson Black moved to Beijing — then known as Peking — and led the push to find and study early human remains there.

Black's enthusiasm for hunting our ancient ancestors steered him away from working as a medical doctor in his home city of Toronto. Instead he taught anatomy at Western Reserve University in Cleveland. Convinced that man had originated in central Asia, he accepted a professorship at Peking Union Medical College in China. From Beijing, Black organized a large-scale search for fossils of prehistoric people. Searchers had found a natural crack inside a limestone cave at Zhoukoudian. There, it was thought, animals and people had fallen to their deaths, or bones were tossed after the tribe had eaten.

Early in the 1900s a German scientist had discovered fossilized human teeth in what were sold as "dragon's bones" by a Peking druggist. (Varied fossils from many locations were called "dragon's bones" in China. They were said to be the remains of extinct giant winged dragons, but no one was really sure what they were.) Traced to the limestone cave, the teeth hinted at important finds in the rock that had filled the crack. Dynamite was used to blast the surrounding rock free, and the rubble was sifted for human remains. Fortunately, a top of a skull was discovered just before winter — and a looming civil war in China — closed the dig.

In 1929, after his field-chief, Dr. Pei Wenzhong, found another partial skull in a nearby site, Dr. Black announced the discovery of Peking Man, a now-extinct species of human. Dated at 300,000 to 500,000 years old, the fossils were older than any European human remains. Other important specimens were found at Zhoukoudian. Plaster casts were carefully made of each fragment. Debates raged about the place of Peking Man in the origin of the human species.

Black died in his Chinese laboratory in 1934. The original fossils were lost when Japanese troops captured a party of United States Marines leaving China in 1941, but the plaster casts remained. Other bones found since then on the same site — fourteen partial skulls, eleven lower jaws, many teeth, some skeletal bones and large numbers of stone tools — add detail to the picture of Peking Man. He was one form of *Homo erectus*, and may have been a cannibal and head-hunter.

Canadian Clean-up

Many useful things are made of plastic. But what happens when we're through with them? Most plastics get thrown into the garbage. Some get washed out to sea. Scientists worry that they don't rot like most garbage — they will still look the same in a hundred, or even a thousand years. Plastic holders for beer packs have killed fish and sea birds by getting stuck over their mouths and beaks. Dolphins and fish drown when they get tangled in plastic nets or ropes. All these plastics floating in the ocean will keep causing harm, because they are unaffected by the sun or salt water. That's a pollution nightmare. We never have to look far to see the problem that plastic litter causes.

There's hope for the future, though, thanks to Dr. James Guillet. He invented degradable plastics — the first environmentally friendly plastics — that turn to dust in sunlight.

The University of Toronto chemist devised his new formula for plastic in 1971. He shared the patent with British researcher Dr. Harvey Troth in 1976. Their new plastic contains molecules sensitive to sunlight. They will decompose when hit by direct — but only direct — sunlight. The same plastics will last indoors on your windowsill because glass partially protects them from sunlight. But when tossed on a roadside they will simply fall apart and turn to dust. This offers some hope for stopping pollution in our parks and oceans — so long as plastics companies decide to use Dr. Guillet's formula.

Guillet's patent was the one millionth Canadian patent issued.

Time Zones Replace Chaos

Until Sir Sandford Fleming persuaded the world to adopt his system of Standard Time Zones, every town and city had its own time zone. When the sun was directly overhead, that was noon. This meant that noon in Kingston was twelve minutes *after* noon in Montreal, and thirteen minutes *before* noon in Toronto. This didn't matter much until people began to travel rapidly from place to place.

In the mid-1800s a railway journey from Halifax, Nova Scotia, to Hamilton, Ontario, required ten changes of a passenger's watch. This made railway schedules difficult, to put it mildly. So railways created their own time zones, but each railway had a different system. To a passenger trying to arrange a journey, it was chaos.

Fleming first proposed Standard Time in 1878. After a lot of research, he suggested dividing the world into twenty-four time zones, with Greenwich, England, as the starting point. Each time zone would be an hour different from the next. At first no one was interested, and some people were actually against this kind of regulation. Fleming's logical and practical system nearly died before it could begin. But Fleming was determined. He never stopped arguing for the advantages of Standard Time, and by 1883 he had finally convinced all the North American railway companies of the worth of his idea.

Fleming spoke to his friend, the Marquis of Lorne, then Governor General of Canada. The Governor General sent an article Fleming had written to all national governments of the world. Russian Czar Nicholas II called for a world conference in Venice in 1884 to discuss Fleming's idea. The twenty-five countries who sent representatives all approved. As a result, Standard Time came into effect on January 1, 1885.

All countries of the world eventually adopted the standard. Canada contains six of the twenty-four time zones. Only the former Soviet Union had more, with nine.

Fleming was knighted for his work on Standard Time, but he was also an important land surveyor in Canada. After Confederation in 1867, Prime Minister John A. Macdonald hired him to do a survey and a study on how Canada could build "A Railway to the Pacific Through British Territory." Fleming began to work toward a trans-Canada railway, coast to coast. He and his team travelled by horseback, by canoe and on foot across wilderness, prairie and mountain ranges to map a route. It was such dangerous work that forty of his men lost their lives. The vast survey made the gigantic task of building such a railway possible. In 1885 Fleming watched as the last spike was driven in to complete the Canadian Pacific Railway. Canada was linked, from sea to sea.

Fleming also designed Canada's first stamp, the "three-penny beaver." The beaver would become a lasting symbol of Canadian wilderness and hard work. Said Fleming, "We do not live for ourselves only, but ... to perform [our duty] to the community."

Can I Use Your Holodeck?

Science fiction inspires real science, as virtual reality (VR) technology advances at breakneck speed. We don't have a *Star Trek* holodeck yet, but we're getting much closer.

The first Java 3-D virtual reality CAVE in the world — the AVE stands for Automatic Virtual Environment — was opened in February, 2002, by the University of Calgary's Faculty of Medicine at the Foothills Hospital. Called the Sun Centre of Excellence for Visual Genomics, the $6 million installation (developed in conjunction with Sun Microsystems Inc.) is the first of its kind. Its function is to let scientists "see the unseen," by surrounding them with three-dimensional larger-than-life biological models. The subject could be anything: an entire human or animal body, an organ, a single cell, or a strand of DNA.

Other versions of the CAVE technology have helped petroleum companies to understand their drilling site's underground landscape better, and helped car manufacturers to perfect their designs and avoid costly mistakes.

Calgary's new medical research facility is expected to help

scientists rapidly obtain a more intricate understanding of highly complex diseases and life processes. Sometimes the chemical and mathematical aspects of life processes are just too complicated for the human mind to visualize clearly, and ordinary computer graphics are limited. Seeing the images in the CAVE shows sometimes surprising relationships between parts of the organisms.

All these applications have one thing in common. VR helps to make clear a vast amount of information, through digital computer imagery. In this case, a 3-D picture is worth a lot more than a thousand words. Interrelationships are revealed in detail. And this facility will be easier to use because of the language used. Since a common programming language — Java 3-D — is used, scientists at remote locations can develop projects for the new lab at home, and just load them in Calgary. They won't have to spend long periods of time creating their applications on-site.

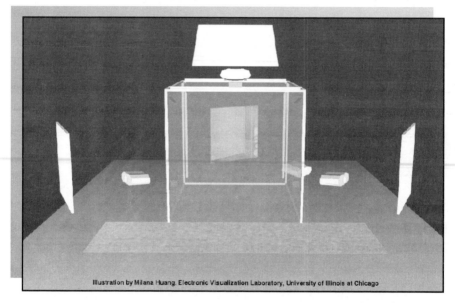

Illustration by Milana Huang, Electronic Visualization Laboratory, University of Illinois at Chicago

The super-powerful computing centre makes the Calgary research team world leaders in bioinformatics — a new research field that maps the complicated information used in biological research. The team will be able to do life-saving research more rapidly. Drug development time should also be reduced. Less time will need to be spent on actual experiments, though of course trials on animals and people will still be needed.

What does a CAVE look like, and how does it work? Large screens instead of walls surround the user on three sides, creating about a 3-metre-square space. The images are projected onto the screens from behind, so the user can get as close to the images as he or she wants. And 3-D glasses are worn to get the entire effect. As the user moves, the super-computers change the viewing angle, imitating real-life vision.

The CAVE technology itself was invented in 1991 by Dan Sandin and Tom DeFanto at the University of Illinois at Chicago's Electronic Visualization Laboratory. In this high-powered technological world, another key player is Kitchener, Ontario's, Fakespace Systems, which sells the CAVEs commercially. Canada's National Research Council, with a VR research CAVE near London, Ontario, is credited with inventing the 3-D laser scanner camera used in the process.

There are more than a hundred CAVEs in use worldwide.

Chocolate to Go

Chocolate — ah, what a treat! So tasty that people dream of it, hoard it, fight over it and go out of their way to get the kind they want. When we get the urge for chocolate, most of us buy a chocolate bar. Protected in its wrappings, it melts in our mouths, not our pockets or backpacks. But the last time you unwrapped a chocolate bar, did you know you were about to bite into a Canadian innovation?

Two men with equal loves for fishing and for chocolate created the wrapped chocolate bar to take along on a fishing trip in 1910. They were Arthur Ganong, of New Brunswick's Ganong candy store, and George Ensor, the Ganong factory superintendent. The delicious chocolates made at the factory were hard to carry on a summer's day — a chocolate bar, wrapped to protect it from the sun, travelled much better.

Ganong and his co-worker quickly realized that others would like their innovation, so they began selling a standard-sized, standard-priced, protectively wrapped five-cent bar — a chocolate-covered confection with nuts and a sweet centre. Safely wrapped, the chocolate was protected against dirt and pocket lint. The Hershey company in the United States had to reach an agreement with Ganong before their first Hershey bars could be manufactured.

Brothers James and Gilbert Ganong, two New Brunswick natives, had begun their candy-making business in 1873. One man was a former jockey, the other a teacher. The brothers also invented the Chicken Bone, a tasty treat having nothing to do with chickens — it's a chocolate-filled hard cinnamon candy. Molded chocolate peppermint rolls originated in the Ganong factory, too, and the Ganongs were the first to sell chocolates in heart-shaped boxes in Canada, forever changing a Valentine's Day tradition. Their hand-dipped chocolates are proudly stamped with the company name to this day, and high quality is their standard. The family business still thrives in St. Stephen, New Brunswick, as Canada's oldest independent candy company.

* The Ganongs opened a soap factory as well, but eventually sold their Surprise Soap recipe to Lever Brothers, where it became Lever 2000.

* People the world over find chocolate irresistible. About 3 million tonnes of chocolate are consumed a year, worldwide.

* Chocolate candy was invented by a Dutch chemist by adding fat and sugar to cocoa. Milk chocolate was first made by a Swiss candy maker who added condensed milk and refined the cocoa's texture — Swiss chocolate is still famous.

* A cocoa press was invented in the eighteenth century, making solid chocolate chunks possible. (Before the chocolate bar, solid chocolate was sold in blocks, rolls and sheets, usually priced by weight.)

* Chocolate is one of the most chemically complex foods, containing about 300 substances, including caffeine, which can act as a stimulant or keep you awake at night.

*Never feed chocolate to your pet. Theobromine and caffeine, both contained in chocolate, are poisonous to cats, dogs and other animals.

What's in the Freezer?

Today we take for granted the ability to get food shipped from far away, including frozen food. In minutes a delicious meal can be taken from the freezer and prepared in the microwave or on the stove. But frozen foods weren't always available to us. In the late 1920s a Canadian marine biologist named Archibald Huntsman got the idea of freezing fish and shipping it to distant markets. He was the first to make it a reality.

Huntsman was working in Halifax for what was to become the federal government's Atlantic Biological Station. At the time, fish could be shipped on ice, but it still might spoil before reaching the dinner table if the ice melted. Huntsman knew frozen fish would keep much, much longer than ice-packed fish. His idea didn't catch on at first, but he pushed it until frozen fish were shipped to Toronto, Montreal, Ottawa and Winnipeg in 1929. The Ice Fillets — frozen fillets of fish ready for the frying pan — were a big success, and more than 50 tonnes of them were sold. "We did it," said Huntsman. "We showed them how." But when the Atlantic Biological Station gave the business to private industry, it floundered. The problem was, in part, lack of finances.

Huntsman was ahead of his time. It wasn't until American inventor Clarence Birdseye invented refrigerated railway cars that the selling of frozen food really took off. Birdseye got the idea of freezing food from watching indigenous people in Labrador . . . but he might have got it from Huntsman, if he had been paying attention.

Today, ships that catch fish can also freeze it, and refrigerated trucks and train cars keep it frozen. Advances in food handling, refrigeration and shipping have revolutionized our daily menu.

Toronto Chemist Invents Canada Dry Ginger Ale

John J. McLaughlin, a graduate of the University of Toronto in chemistry and pharmacy, created the number one ginger ale in the world. McLaughlin owned a drugstore in Toronto in the late 1800s. In the 1890s he began making soft drinks, juice and ice cream in a new plant in Toronto. By bottling soft drinks, he made it possible for people to buy them and take them home, instead of just drinking them in his store.

The temperance movement — people speaking out against the evils of alcohol — was in full swing in Toronto at the time, so McLaughlin decided to invent a non-alcoholic ginger ale. (In Ireland, ginger ale *was* an alcoholic beer. You'll still get served ginger beer if you ask for ginger ale there.) McLaughlin tinkered with an old Irish recipe for ten years and in 1904 produced his first ginger ale soft drink — McLaughlin Belfast Style Ginger Ale. His customers found it too sweet, so more tinkering followed. By 1905 he had made it lighter and much less sweet and renamed it Canada Dry Pale Ginger Ale, borrowing the word "dry" from the wine industry, to mean less sugar content. The new recipe was an overnight success.

McLaughlin patented the secret recipe in 1907. (It's still a secret. Reportedly, only three people in the world know it.) His booming sales took off even more after the Governor General of Canada appointed Canada Dry products to his Royal Household. That gave McLaughlin permission to use a crown and shield on the Canada Dry label.

McLaughlin wasn't just a clever inventor. He proved to be a marketing genius. The slogan "The Champagne of Ginger Ales" was a winner, giving the beverage an upper-class image.

McLaughlin died in 1914, but his brothers took over the business and built on its success. Canada Dry products now sell in 90 countries on six continents — a sensational market success. But all of that hardly matters when you have a queasy stomach and your doctor recommends lots of ginger ale and bed rest. Thank you, McLaughlin!

In the early 1950s, Canada Dry was the first major soft drink company to put soft drinks in cans. Canada Dry "cone" cans are worth up to $85 each to collectors today. Canada Dry led the way in sugar-free soft drinks, too, in the mid-1960s.

One Canadian Tree Spawns a Dynasty

Every McIntosh apple you eat today can trace its roots back to a single tree. Over 3 million trees in North America are descended from that one tree found growing wild on John McIntosh's Ontario farm in 1811. Today's scientists call the apparently accidental creation of the McIntosh apple a one-in-a-million chance. Nature created the apple; settler McIntosh found it, transplanted it and grew it; his son Alan spread it far and wide.

Apples were first brought from Normandy, France, to Port Royal, Nova Scotia, in 1606. John McIntosh came to Canada about 200 years later. After quarreling with his parents over a love affair, McIntosh left their New York State farm and headed north to Canada. Here he married and settled on his own farm. This much we know. The origin of the trees McIntosh found is more of a mystery.

Part of McIntosh's farm at Dundela, in eastern Ontario, had been cleared by a previous settler. When McIntosh himself cleared a small section of second-growth forest, about 3 metres high, to build his own house, he discovered several young apple trees. Since they were in the second growth, they must have been accidentally seeded from the first settler's trees. Apples were hard to come by, and were often the only fruit on a pioneer farm. McIntosh transplanted the small trees into his garden. Only one survived. When it produced fruit at last, McIntosh found the apples to be the best he had ever tasted. They were firm, juicy and sweet — good for eating, drying, cooking and preserving. His apples were soon famous in the district.

Every neighbour wanted an apple tree like McIntosh's, but like most apple trees, its seeds did not breed true. The tree was unique until a wandering hired hand showed the family how to graft apple trees — attaching a branch of their tree to another apple tree. It was the only way to share their apple wealth. The grafted trees produced true McIntosh apples — all the branches that grew above the graft were genetically identical to the original McIntosh tree.

John McIntosh's son Alan started a tree nursery. Every spring he set out with a sack full of McIntosh cuttings and branches on his back. He spread the tree through eastern Ontario, New York and Vermont, and from there it travelled even farther afield. Today apples are the most important fruit (in dollar value) grown in Canada.

And the original tree? McIntosh's house burned down in the mid-1890s. The tree was badly scorched. It bore its last harvest in 1908 and died two years later. Its many offspring live on.

The Maple Tree Forever

Canada is the world leader in maple syrup production. In the year 2000, over 40,000 tonnes of maple syrup were made here, worth an estimated $151.5 million at the farm gates. Wow! That's more than 85 percent of the world's maple syrup production, with the United States making up the other 15 percent. Quebec sap tappers make most of Canada's syrup — over 93 percent. Ontario, New Brunswick and Nova Scotia produce the remainder. More than half of Canada's maple syrup gets sold to other countries, primarily the United States, for over a hundred million dollars. It's no wonder we see maple syrup bottles in souvenir shops. Other parts of the world don't have this sweet treat because they just don't have the right kind of maple trees.

Maple syrup gets made in March and April. Sugar maples, red maples and silver maples are tapped for their sweet sap. When European explorers landed in Canada, they found indigenous people collecting the sap in birchbark buckets. Now it is collected mainly by tubes and vacuum pumps, then boiled down to concentrate it. Some of the tree's nutrients are used up to make syrup, but maple sugar bush farmers are careful to keep their trees healthy.

Why only maple trees? All trees have sap. Starch made in the leaves during the previous growing season is changed to sugar in the spring. But maple sap is sweeter than other trees' sap and has that winning flavour. An average maple tree gives between 35 and 50 litres of sap annually; about 40 litres are needed to make a single litre of syrup.

Maple syrup contains a few more nutrients than refined sugar (such as calcium, thiamin and riboflavin). But that's not why we enjoy eating it. We eat it because it tastes so good! Not all of it gets poured on pancakes, either. Some of it is added to cereals, yogurts and other foods as a sweetener.

In the 1960s, producers of maple syrup couldn't make enough. The labour-intensive sap-tapping methods of the past were impractical, and in some areas as much as 70 percent of the maple sugar bush was left untapped. A new method of collecting the sap was needed. Denis Dislets of Laval University invented a vacuum tubing system, which helped the sap flow more easily, in larger quantities, and with better quality. The system also delivered the sap to the evaporator via tubing, so no one had to collect it in buckets by hand. The invention put many maple syrup producers back in business, and the sap has been flowing every spring ever since.

The Cereal that Saved Lives

A hospital was the unlikely birthplace of the world's first pre-cooked breakfast food for infants — Pablum. Milk alone is not enough for a baby past early infancy. Even mother's milk doesn't have the iron a baby needs for healthy growth. But baby foods were difficult to prepare in the 1920s, and few parents knew the best combination of foods to use. Mushy versions of a perfect diet didn't exist, so the first solid foods given to babies often lacked important vitamins, minerals and protein. Around 1930 three doctors at The Hospital for Sick Children in Toronto set out to make the perfect food for babies. They kept at it until the food was properly balanced and could be made quickly. The result, Pablum, has helped millions of children in Canada and around the world grow up healthy.

It all began when Dr. Alan Brown, the Toronto-born physician-in-charge at The Hospital for Sick Children, grew concerned about the number of babies dying in the hospital. He thought a poor diet might be part of the reason. He assigned the job of making a complete food for babies to Dr. Theodore Drake and Dr. Frederick Tisdall, specialists in nutrition at the hospital. It wasn't easy, but Brown pushed the project through with his iron determination. They created the ideal baby food, and it became the standard food used in the hospital.

Pablum is made from wheat meal, oatmeal, cornmeal, wheat germ, bone meal, dried brewer's yeast and alfalfa — foods carried by health food stores today, but little known back then, when refined white flour and white bread dominated North American markets. The doctors named their invention after the Latin word *pabulum*, which means *fodder* or *food for the mind*.

Dr. Brown's reforms in the hospital, including the introduction of Pablum, helped more infants survive and grow into healthy adults. Brown also urged mothers to breast-feed their babies, in an era when it was rare to do so in North America. The death rate for babies went down dramatically.

Pablum is easy to prepare. Parents need only add milk or water and serve it hot or cold. When Pablum hit the market in 1931 it was an instant hit, not just in Canada but around the world. It didn't need to be refrigerated or frozen. It kept its nutritional value a long time, stored dry.

For twenty-five years, for every box of Pablum sold, a few cents went to The Hospital for Sick Children. These royalties mounted up into a lot of money, which was used to fund research at the hospital. Countless improvements in the care of sick children were financed by Pablum, and helped make the hospital one of the leading children's hospitals in the world.

Doctors Drake and Tisdall were nutritional advisors to many groups, including the Canadian Armed Forces. Dr. Tisdall also improved the standards of food given out in soup kitchens during the Depression. Prisoners of war had a lot to thank him for, too — he began the custom of sending food parcels to them through the Red Cross.

Today you can still find Pablum on the grocer's shelves. It may be bland in flavour, but in an emergency, it would be hard to find a more perfect food. And babies still thrive on it.

What a Flake!

Foods in flake or powdered form — they don't need to be refrigerated, canned or frozen; they are easy and fast to prepare by adding water or milk. Most of the work is done ahead of time, by the process that makes the flake. Dr. Edward Asselbergs and his research group at the Food Research Institute in Ottawa produced instant powdered foods in the early 1960s. They were freeze-dried ground meat, cheese, fish and potatoes.

The scientists first began the project because northern Europe was short of high-protein food. Few households there had refrigerators, so they needed foods that wouldn't spoil. Freeze-dried food could be easily shipped, too. By the time the research and development were completed, however, conditions in Europe had improved enough that flaked foods weren't so necessary. Still, instant mashed potatoes made it to Canadian and American grocery shelves, and were popular for a while. The flakes didn't taste like freshly mashed potatoes, even after milk and butter were added, but they were convenient.

Newer versions of instant mashed potatoes taste a lot better than the original version. Even though many families prefer a frozen potato product today for convenience, potato flakes continue to be an important ingredient in other dried foods. They keep dried meat or cheese from lumping together. You'd never even know the potato flakes were in there if you didn't read the label. Instant cheese is still part of a popular macaroni and cheese dinner.

Campers and the military use freeze-dried foods because they are light to carry, won't spoil in any kind of weather, and, if sealed, don't need to be kept cold. Meals for a week weigh very little, since it's the water in foods that weighs so much. Relief agencies ship dried foods to disaster or famine zones around the world.

The Wheat That Won the West

In 1843 a farmer in Peterborough, Ontario, David Fife, was conducting experiments to find a new strain of wheat, because Canadian summers were too short for most wheat to grow to maturity. That year Fife's trial crop died, except for three plants — and those were saved only because his wife prevented a stray cow from eating them! From those few survivors, Red Fife wheat was bred. The strain ripened ten days earlier than any other known type of wheat. It was also high-yielding, and excellent for bread-making. Red Fife wheat was a major breakthrough, but even so, crops were often lost on the prairies. Farmers were slow to settle in the Canadian West because of the short growing season.

In 1886 William Saunders became the first director of the Dominion Experimental Farms in Ottawa. He tried to cross Red Fife with other wheats to make a more disease-resistant variety, still suitable to Canada's climate. With the help of Saunders' sons, Percy and Charles, over 700 varieties were tested. Percy Saunders had originally crossed Red Fife with an East Indian variety, Hard Red Calcutta wheat, but the results were still uneven. William Saunders asked Charles to continue the effort.

Charles Saunders refined the strain his father had tried (originally called Markham) until its best characteristics ran true. The resulting wheat was called Marquis. It was ready for harvest in 100 days — a week to ten days earlier than even Red Fife. Early frosts on the prairies destroyed many other varieties of wheat, but not Marquis. In 1907, after years of trials, it was ready for testing by farmers. Many other crops were lost to early frosts that year, but the Marquis wheat was ready for harvest in time. With an even higher yield than Red Fife and more disease resistance, Marquis was a winner. In 1908 farmers flocked to buy Marquis seeds. Within a decade, 90 percent of the wheat planted in the Canadian West was Marquis. In 1911 it was awarded the gold prize at the World's Fair in New York, as the best wheat grown anywhere in the world.

After these developments, farmers in the Canadian West didn't just survive. They flourished. Canada became one of the main bread baskets of the world; the wheat industry now generates billions of dollars. Several other successful strains of wheat were produced by Charles Saunders too — Ruby, Garnet and Reward — all specially adapted to the prairies.

Charles Saunders suffered ill health, and retired on a meagre pension. He lived in poverty for a while, but he had made such a huge impact on western farming practices that farmers demanded the government recognize him. The first "Dominion cerealist," he was given a lifetime pension by the federal government, in recognition of his contribution to the country. He was later knighted.

To this day Canada remains one of the leading producers of wheat in the world. Without Red Fife wheat and Saunders, that would have been impossible. Said the shy, methodical Charles Saunders, "Anyone could have done the same."

Safer Meat To Come

Canadian researchers are testing a new vaccine on cattle, one that attacks *E. coli* bacteria in live animals. (*E. coli* is a type of bacteria found in animal manure.) In late 2001, trials began on thousands of cows in Alberta. The vaccine leads to a much lower *e. coli* count in cattle manure — a thousandfold less.

Why worry about *E. coli*? Seven people died and thousands became ill when rain washed bacteria from cattle manure into municipal wells at Walkerton, Ontario, in early May of 2000. Drinking water from the contaminated wells infected people with *E. coli* and *Campylobacter jejuni* bacteria. Other *E. coli* victims have become ill after eating contaminated meat — improperly handled ground beef has been a carrier for the bacteria — or berries and vegetables irrigated with contaminated water. But with cleaner cattle, the problem will be much easier to handle — fewer bacteria, less hazard.

Dr. Brett Finlay, Professor of Biotechnology at the University of British Columbia, developed a cattle vaccine that, it is hoped, will greatly reduce the problem at the source, instead of trying to clean it up or contain it later. The Veterinary Infectious Disease Organization studied the vaccine and found that it worked well. The Alberta Research Council will produce the vaccine at its Edmonton plant. Clinical studies will continue at Bioniche Life Sciences Inc., a Belleville, Ontario, drug company.

Dr. Colin O. Gill, a research scientist at the Agriculture and Agri-Food Canada Research Centre in Lacombe, Alberta, has also come up with a cleaner way to deal with beef during processing. He worked with Edmonton's Stanfos, Inc. to develop an award-winning system of hot-water carcass pasteurization. In February of 2001 he reported results of trials with another pasteurization process for beef trimmings. The beef destined for your burger is treated again with hot water at 85°C for 60 seconds. The one-minute treatment rids the beef of all *E. coli* that might have been introduced during the processing stages. Stanfos tested the prototype again, with great success.

Safer food production is closer than ever. Now you just have to remember to wash your hands.

The Lentil Basket of the World?

This isn't the kind of news you hear about every day: Canada is the world's largest exporter of lentils.

Lentils. You know, those flat little green, brown or red pea-like or bean-like veggie things officially called "pulses." You've probably eaten them in soups, salads or stews. They are tasty, too. They're very virtuous, lentils — high in vegetable protein and fibre, low in fat. In the year 2000 alone, about 914,000 tonnes of lentils were grown, chiefly in Saskatchewan. Over half of that was exported to India, Bangladesh and Spain, but an amazingly large number of them got eaten here. Keep a lookout.

Soy What?

A few decades ago few people in Canada knew what tofu was. Now we grow soybeans and make a world-quality tofu right here.

Soybeans wouldn't even grow in Canada until Agriculture and Agri-Food Canada developed Harosoy and other quick-maturing strains. Now soybeans are grown on almost 1 million hectares of land across Canada, with 87 percent of today's $670 million crop grown in Ontario. Most of it is used to make soy drinks, tofu and miso (a fermented bean paste). Bred for high protein content, the bean products are chiefly exported to Asia, where they represent a major source of vegetable protein.

From Industrial Oil to Classy Food

During World War II, rapeseed was grown in Canada for use as a substitute industrial oil. The lowly seed was bred into a more useful one by scientists in Agriculture and Agri-Food Canada, with the help of the National Research Council. They called the new seed canola, and pressed it for high quality edible oil and animal feed.

Canola crops were first grown in the 1970s. Canola took the prairies by storm, to become a crop second only to wheat. You've probably eaten canola oil in everything from margarine to granola bars.

Spider Silk from a Goat? — Food That's, Well, Not Food

What's more flexible and five times stronger than steel? Give up? Spider silk.

About 100 million years ago, spiders developed the ability to spin their amazing silk-like fibre. One-tenth the thickness of a human hair, spider silk can still stop a speeding bee. It's stronger than man-made fibres like Kevlar. It's 25 percent lighter than synthetic fibres, which are usually made from petroleum. For some time scientists have been on a quest to find a way to produce enough "spider fibre" to be used commercially. It's superior and environmentally friendly as well. When it's left behind, spider fibre rots and disappears, unlike plastic fishing line, for example, that will hang around for decades, perhaps centuries, and become a tangled hazard for fish and marine mammals. Spider fibre fishing nets would eventually decay, and be unlikely to strangle a dolphin or kill a whale. Spider silk might also be used to create tough, strong tendons and ligaments for injured people.

So why not get together large numbers of spiders, set them spinning, and harvest what industry needs? Silk worms are farmed for their silk — why not spiders? There's a problem: Even for those who like the eight-legged creatures, spiders aren't good farming livestock. They're too anti-social to like living together in groups. To put it bluntly, they eat their neighbours.

To overcome this hurdle, scientists at Nexia Biotechnologies in Quebec got busy. They introduced genes from spiders into goats. (Genes tell a cell, basically, how to develop.) Did the scientists come up with a sci-fi monster? No. The goats they produced — the first cloned goats were named Webster and Pete — looked like any other.

But there was one big difference. Webster and Pete were the world's first goats to carry spider genes. By January of 2002 there was a herd of fifty spider-goats. The gene for spider silk was successfully passed on to goat offspring.

So far, so good.

But how can a goat make spider fibre? It can't. However, the way a goat (or any mammal) makes proteins for milk is roughly the same way spiders make silk proteins. Proteins from these special goats' milk were removed and spun into "spider fibre." It was tough and could stretch without breaking.

At the time of *Made in Canada*'s publication, this project is still in the developmental stage. The goat's milk fibre is only 20 to 40 percent as strong as natural spider silk. And at least 200 "transgenic" goats would be required to fulfill world demand for the goat silk. But biodegradable fishing line and super-fine suture fibre to use in surgical operations might be available in the near future. Other applications "on the drawing board" are things like lightweight body armour.

Waterproof Telegraph Lines Link Distant Places

It's 1850. Imagine you're taking the train to visit your aunt in Ottawa. Arrangements have been made by letter. But your train has broken down. How can you let your aunt know, so she won't wait at the station for hours? The telephone hasn't been invented, but you can go to the telegraph office and pay to have your message sent by telegraph (the word means "to write far"). A telegraph operator, using Morse code, sends your message over a wire. Since every word costs money, it pays to shorten your message. It might read, "Train delayed STOP Will arrive tomorrow same time STOP." (The word "STOP" was used to separate sentences.) In your aunt's town, another operator will listen to the dots and dashes of Morse code and write out the message in words on paper. The message will then be delivered, probably by a boy or man on a bicycle. But what if you want to "talk" to your grandmother in England? Impossible. Telegraph wires are strung over land only. There is no way to send a message across the Atlantic Ocean, except by ship.

Engineer Frederick Newton Gisborne of St. John's, Newfoundland, saw the solution. He experimented with underwater communication cables. Using an insulated wire that could not be damaged by salt water, he laid a telegraph cable from New Brunswick to Prince Edward Island in 1852, the first submarine cable in North America. Then Gisborne succeeded in linking St. John's, Newfoundland, to New Brunswick. The section of the line that crossed land covered 640 kilometres of Newfoundland wilderness, and nearly bankrupted Gisborne. Cyrus Field, an American industrialist, financed the ongoing work, so the undersea section to Cape Breton (necessary to eventually reach New Brunswick) could be completed. Gisborne's next vision was on an even bigger scale. Why not lay a wire from Newfoundland across the North Atlantic to Ireland?

The idea sounds fantastic even today. It wasn't easy, but Field was convinced of Gisborne's plan, and he invested again. The first attempt to bridge the Atlantic by cable in 1857 failed, but an attempt in the summer of 1858 succeeded in linking Ireland with Newfoundland. The cable was laid by carefully playing it out from a ship and splicing cables together whenever one reel of cable ran out.

The first message, sent on August 16, 1858, read, "Europe and America are united by telegraphy. Glory to God in the Highest, on earth peace, goodwill toward men." It did seem like a miracle . . . until the cable failed within two months. It must have sprung a leak or broken somewhere along its length, but no one knew where. A reliable cable was finally installed in July of 1866.

Gisborne didn't lay the final cable, but his was the drive that had started the project and the pioneering work that made the cable salt-water resistant — making the Trans-Atlantic Cable possible.

The Telephone Was Invented Where?

Citizens of the United States claim the telephone as their invention. Canadians insist it's ours. What's the true story? Alexander Graham Bell emigrated from Scotland to Canada with his family in 1870. Later he worked in the United States. He was travelling back and forth between Canada and the United States during the period when he invented the telephone.

Bell had the idea of the telephone while visiting his father in Brantford, Ontario, in 1874. There he made an "ear phono autograph" from a stalk of hay and a dead man's ear. (Ears helped him understand hearing in his work with the deaf — Bell's lifelong passion.) When he spoke into the ear, the haystalk traced the sound waves on a piece of smoked glass. Bell suddenly realized that speech produced sound waves that could be carried by electrical wires.

Bell knew he could make a device with a soft iron diaphragm that would vibrate with sound waves, like the eardrum does. Those vibrations would affect the field of a nearby magnet, which would then create changes in the electrical current in a thin wire wrapped around the magnet. These changes in the electrical current's intensity could be relayed to another longer wire, which could then be strung along poles to a distant location. There the electrical signal could be transformed into sound again by a similar magnetic device, with its own diaphragm. Later, improved versions of the telephone employed the same basic principles. Bell built the first telephone in Boston, Massachusetts, in 1875. His first words carried by the device are famous today. On March 12, 1875, he called to his assistant, who was located in another room of the same house, "Mr. Watson. Come here. I want to see you."

The first telephone call from one building to another was made between two Ontario towns — Mount Pleasant and Brantford — on August 3, 1876. One week later, the first long-distance call was made between Brantford and Paris, Ontario, over a 13-kilometre distance.

Bell had also been trying to improve the telegraph system. He wrote to his father, "The day is coming when telegraph wires will be laid on to houses just like water or gas — and friends will converse with each other without leaving home." His notebooks are filled with predictions as futuristic and (at the time) unlikely as this one. But that day came during his own lifetime. Telephone lines were installed very quickly so that Bell's invention could be used by the public.

While Bell lived and taught in Boston, he returned to Canada often. At his summer home in Baddeck, on Cape Breton Island, Nova Scotia, he worked on his many inventions. There he spent the last thirty-six years of his life. (Bell stuffed a towel around his own telephone in Baddeck. "I never use the beast," he said of it.)

Bell's advice to other inventors was, "Leave the beaten track occasionally and dive into the woods. Every time you do so you will be certain to find something that you have never seen before."

Controversy over the telephone's invention still rages. In June of 2002 the United States Congress passed a resolution stating that a poor Italian immigrant to New York, Antonio Meucci, developed a telephone prototype before Bell did. The Italian Historical Society of America found Meucci's story. They claim he had a working prototype in 1855, linking his home to his nearby workshop. Meucci filed notice of his patent in 1871, but he didn't have the $10 to renew his notice in 1874. If he had, Bell would not have been able to file his own U.S. patent in 1876. Meucci died before his case for the invention of the telephone could be resolved.

Bell defended his patent more than 600 times in court. Canada's House of Commons passed its own motion recognizing Bell as the inventor of the telephone, in response to the United States' Congressional claim.

* Other inventors seemed to have had ideas similar to Bell's. Elisha Gray filed an intent to patent the phone just hours before Bell's patent was filed. First with the actual patent, Bell won out. And German historians claim Philipp Reis invented a telephone in 1861, but Germany had no patent laws to protect the invention.

* Bell's father and grandfather were noted speech experts. His mother, Eliza Bell, was deaf. Bell was proudest of his work teaching the deaf to speak. One of his students was Helen Keller, and another student later became his wife.

* Bell's other inventions numbered over 100. With a small group he also developed the first Canadian aircraft, the Silver Dart. Bell came up with the idea for the aileron, too — the hinged section of an aircraft's wing that makes flight corrections — and tricycle landing gears for planes. He was a co-founder of *National Geographic Magazine*, and president of the National Geographic Society from 1895 to 1904.

The Forgotten Father of Radio

In the 1880s Reginald A. Fessenden told Thomas Edison that human speech could be sent through the air without wires. Edison laughed. After all, Fessenden had come from Canada to Edison's plant to learn *from* the famous American inventor. Edison tried to set the dreamer straight. "Fezzie, what do you say are man's chances of jumping over the moon? I figure that one is about as likely as the other." It seemed that Edison was right — in those days the best communication was by Morse code sent over wires: the telegraph.

But Edison was wrong. Using the first wireless station — built using Fessenden's own design, two 15-metre-high telegraph masts and another tower 80 kilometres away — he sent the world's first successful wireless voice transmission on December 23, 1900. He said, "One, two, three, four. [Is it] snowing where you are, Mr. Thiessen? If it is, telegraph back and let me know." Over a kilometre and a half away, Fessenden's assistant did so, proving that the test worked. (It *was* snowing.) The experiment took place near Washington, D.C., where the Quebec-born Fessenden was working.

Following this triumph, Fessenden applied to the Canadian government for funding, but was turned down. His invention seemed too far-fetched. Besides, Canada had already given the patent for radio, as well as funding, to Italian Guglielmo Marconi (then working in both Canada and in Great Britain), who could transmit Morse code through the air. Marconi received the first wireless sound signal — a buzz — at Signal Hill in St. John's, Newfoundland, from Cornwall, England. Marconi had the world's ear. He captured the imagination of people, even though Fessenden could send *spoken* words when Marconi could send only buzzes.

Denied by Canada, Fessenden sought out two millionaires in Pittsburgh for backing. With that in place he proceeded with the invention of the heterodyne, which combines sound frequencies and so forms the basis of all radio transmission. For six years Fessenden refined his technique, developing a high-frequency alternator as part of his transmitter. He also built two towers, each 120 metres tall, to house his radio stations — one off the coast of Massachusetts, the other on the coast of Scotland. In December of 1906 he transmitted a Christmas concert from Boston to ships in the Caribbean — the first radio program in the world. He read the Bible, sang, played "O Holy Night" on his violin and played a phonograph recording. The ships' crews were astonished.

Fessenden's staggering accomplishment changed our lives forever. The age of mass communication had begun. By 1922 there were 600 commercial broadcasting stations in the United States alone. Yet Fessenden is seldom remembered as radio's pioneer.

Fessenden understood concepts that other scientists wouldn't discover for years. He was far ahead of his time. While everyone thought sound was like a whiplash — short sharp bursts of energy — he believed it was like waves, rippling outward in all directions. His theory would later be called the theory of amplitude modulation.

As stubborn as he was brilliant, the flamboyant Fessenden would not give up on his radical ideas. He lost his job when Edison laid him off during a financial crunch. He taught at American universities and then founded his own company to develop his inventions, but he fought with his partners and left the company. They responded by selling his patents — without his permission — to the Radio Corporation of America (RCA). Fessenden sued and the court battles went on for many years. Finally he got an out-of-court settlement of $2.5 million.

Said the *New York Herald Tribune* at Fessenden's death in 1932, "It sometimes happens, even in science, that one man can be right against the world. Professor Fessenden was that man. He fought bitterly and alone to prove his theories." Fessenden's gravestone in Bermuda reads, "By his genius, distant lands converse and men sail unafraid upon the Deep."

Fessenden invented the heterodyne, which converts radio signals into a controllable frequency that can be amplified (made louder) and heard by our ears. He went on to patent 500 inventions in all. Shocked by the sinking of the *Titanic* and the terrible loss of life, he invented radio sonar to allow ships to detect underwater hazards like icebergs and rocks, and so avoid collisions with objects hidden beneath the sea. He invented the depth-sounder, which tells ships accurately how deep the water is below them. The list goes on — turbo electric drive for ships, the wireless compass and the electro-gyro compass for submarines. In 1927 Fessenden even received an American patent for an early form of television! He said, "The real thing is not in the moment of invention but in the preparation which led up to it."

A One-Man Revolution in Radio

Radio power was unreliable until Toronto's Edward Samuel Rogers came along in the 1920s. The heavy batteries that powered home radios sometimes failed in the middle of a broadcast. But batteries were necessary because radios couldn't run on household electricity at that time, since it used an alternating current, while radios ran on direct current. (Alternating current created a deafening hum through a radio tube.)

Rogers invented a radio tube with special filters that could operate from alternating current, then invented a radio that could be plugged in without problems. He called this "the batteryless radio." Engineers were sure he would fail, but he was determined. He studied a great deal and worked for hours and hours each day in his laboratory, spending a full year on the problem before filing his patent in 1925.

Rogers Experimental 15-S. The world's first AC-tube, 1925.

Rogers and his father became partners and created a radio manufacturing company, then went on to form their own radio station, CFRB (Canada's First Rogers Batteryless). CFRB was the first station to broadcast with alternating — versus direct — current. By himself Rogers had ushered in a new age in radio entertainment. CFRB's radio transmissions, begun in 1927, were clearer and more powerful, with bigger and better shows than the five other Toronto radio stations. In the 1930s Rogers was awarded one of the first licenses to experiment with television in Canada.

Rogers's family should have seen it coming. He had spent his boyhood in the family attic, building and operating a homemade telegraph "wireless" station. In 1914 he announced the beginning of World War I before the local newspapers did — he had heard the short-wave announcement from Britain. In 1921 he was the first Canadian amateur to transmit a radio signal across the Atlantic.

Edward S. Rogers died suddenly in 1939. His son, Ted Rogers Jr., carried on in the business and created a communications empire. He says of his father, "Whatever he did, he gave it his very best. He often worked all night in the radio plant, developing new ideas. He was overworked by the time he was thirty-nine, the year of his death."

Rogers's five-tube "Rogers Batteryless" radio offered convenience and quality sound for $260 plus a $45 speaker — a very large price tag in the 1920s. Despite its high price, the Rogers Radio sold well. It was the best available at the time.

The Spy Master Who Created Telephotos

Today we can literally watch the news unfold in another part of the world, as television journalists report from the scene. In newspapers we see photos of events only hours old. The world is a global village, where we know the problems and triumphs of every country, where we are moved to action, such as rushing food or medicines to starving or sick people. That can only happen because dedicated reporters bring us news so rapidly and vividly. Without William Stephenson's invention, none of this would be possible. He found a way to transmit photographs clearly by radio.

Before Stephenson's invention, photos could be sent by wire. Canadians William Leggo and George Desbarats had created a way to print photographs using the dot matrix method, one that is still used today. Such photos were a little fuzzy, but were a tremendous advance over drawings. Still, where wires didn't go, photographs didn't go, except in someone's hand or by mail. A train or even a plane wasn't fast enough for hot news items. Only radio transmission could do that. When Stephenson invented the telephoto, a whole new kind of news was born. Newspapers could print photos of sensational faraway events in the next edition.

In 1924 the very first telephoto appeared in England's *London Daily Mail*. Unlike earlier rough attempts, the photo was crisp and clear. At the sender's end, Stephenson's device used a photo-electric cell and two whirling disks to break down the image into uniform-sized dots of variable darkness, from very light to black, then into electric impulses. Transmitted by telephone or radio, the impulses helped to create a crisp photo using a similar device at the receiver's end.

Stephenson had begun working on telephoto transmission in 1921 when he was teaching at the University of Manitoba. Canadian newspapers weren't interested in his idea, though, so he went to England, where he perfected his invention and patented it in 1922. Soon all the large newspapers of the world were using his technique — one that paved the way for television and fax machines, which both use the same principle. Stephenson became a millionaire by the time he was thirty. But his most famous career was yet to come.

Stephenson is now better known by his World War II nickname — Intrepid. He was knighted for his war efforts, which involved coordinating spy services (secret service and counter-espionage) for England in North and South America. At one point in the war, Stephenson controlled all four major British Intelligence departments, including MI-5. He directed the work to break enemy codes, uncover enemy spies and train field agents for the Allies. He set up Camp X in Oshawa, Ontario, where agents for the Allies got basic training. Graduates included actors Cary Grant and David Niven, Canadian Prime Minister Lester Pearson and writer Ian Fleming. Fleming, the creator of the famous James Bond novels, may have based his master spy character, M, on Stephenson.

The Java Revolution

Do you use the Internet? Then you've probably used Java, a computer programming language that turns plain Web pages into powerful tools. Web pages had text and pictures before Java, but Java makes it possible to run powerful software inside a Web page. Java can turn Web pages into video games, chat rooms or on-line banking terminals, even though the page is being opened on different types of computers or even on cellular phones. How can Web creators be sure their pages will work when most software can only run on the type of computer it's designed for?

Programming whiz James Gosling invented Java so that different machines could run the same software — but he didn't know it would revolutionize the way we buy a book, do our banking and "chat" with friends. Java is a new generation computer language that includes most of the best features of previous languages but fixes many of the problems that make software slow to write and buggy. Gosling's big innovation was to have the computer opening the Web page perform the final processing of the software and customize it for that computer, which is the key to allowing Java programs to run on any kind of system. Java also includes important security measures that help insure someone can't write Web pages that steal credit card numbers or private documents from your computer.

Why did Gosling invent the ultimate computer "translation" system? He wanted to create more friendly computer systems, ones non-experts could easily use. In 1991 he envisioned a programming language any small computer — for example, a Palm Pilot — could understand. When the World Wide Web exploded on the scene, Gosling's universal computer language quickly moved in, because Java was the perfect tool to turn Web pages into sophisticated communication and data processing tools. By 1996 orders had mounted into the millions per year.

How did Gosling get so good? He always loved gadgets. At the age of twelve he made an electronic tic-tac-toe game with parts from an old telephone and television. Gosling himself says he got his education by "break-in." While living on a farm near Calgary, he soon discovered the mainframe computer at the University of Calgary. He was only fourteen when he broke into the mainframe, by sneaking into physics classes to use the terminals. He taught himself how to use it to create computer programs. He was still in high school when the university hired him to write software. Eventually Gosling earned his university degree the usual way.

Gosling lives in California now. He thinks about linking business computers with office equipment, suppliers and contractors. Java can link home computers with the tiny computer brains in cars, stoves, microwave ovens, VCRs, alarm systems and more. The "smart" house, once a dream in Gosling's mind, is already becoming a reality.

Tuning Out TV Violence

A Canadian tragedy led directly to the development of the V-chip (the V stands for "viewer"), a technology that allows parents to keep their children from viewing certain programs, even when the parent isn't home.

On December 6, 1989, Marc Lepine shot fourteen women to death and wounded others at l'École Polytechnique in Montreal. Canadians were horrified. Tim Collings, an electrical engineering professor at Simon Fraser University in British Columbia, watched the newscasts in his home and listened as commentators made references to Lepine's love of violent videos, and the possible influence of television violence. The references caught Collings's imagination. If technology had helped create this problem, technology should help solve it, he reasoned.

Collings began to read extensively on the subject. He became convinced that television violence was implicated in increasing crime levels. In 1990 he began working toward a possible home-based solution, where parents could take responsibility and some control over the television-viewing habits of their children.

Various television industry representatives formed the Action Group on Violence on Television in 1993. Television program classifications looked like the way to protect young children against television violence in Canada, without loss of artistic freedom. The Canadian Radio-Television and Telecommunications Commission (CRTC) ruled in favour of such a classification system in 1996. When the Action Group on Violence on Television (AGVOT), a volunteer non-profit organization, finalized the classifications in 1997, Collings had the V-chip ready to complete the system. Nationwide field trials of V-chip technology, and classification codes, took place that year.

The first V-chips were enclosed in a box attached to television sets. Parents liked the V-chip, but wanted it built into TVs for easier use. Until that could happen, broadcasters agreed to use ratings icons and on-air warnings about program content to keep viewers informed. Televisions including the V-chip have been phased in by manufacturers. All new TV sets in Canada and the United States are now required to have them. Early 2002 estimates put the number of V-chip-equipped sets in Canadian homes at 200,000 and growing. Kits to retro-fit older televisions are also available.

How does it work? There are six levels to the English Canadian rating system, plus an Exempt classification for programs where freedom of information is protected, such as newscasts. Movies have their own system of ratings. The codes are carried in a part of the television signal you normally don't see. Parents set the dis-allowed classifications, and lock in their choices using an identifica-tion number. They can "turn off" the V-chip for their own viewing.

The V-chip has given both resources and information to parents who wish to reduce the violence their children see on television. For his work, Collings has received numerous awards.

Arms You Can Trust

Moving things around in outer space is no small task. First of all, there's no air to breathe. The temperature is cold enough to make normal metal brittle. There's no easy place to stand, and the objects needing to be moved might be huge and hard to grab. But they might also be so delicate that they can easily break . . . and they can be very expensive. There is no room for error. So how are objects moved? A few tiny objects might be shifted by an astronaut in full protective gear on a rope tether — a costly and dangerous task. To really get the job done, and done safely, a super-sized arm, immune to the harsh conditions of outer space, would be ideal. So Canada built one — the Canadarm, our contribution to NASA, and then to the international space program.

It took the first Canadarm, the Shuttle Remote Manipulator System designed in the 1970s, to unload Canadarm2, the new Space Station Remote Manipulator System. Then the first Canadarm attached Canadarm2 to a lab named Destiny on the International Space Station. The historic event, including the first ever "hand-shake" between the two robotic arms, took place in April of 2001, about 400 kilometres above the earth. Canadian astronaut Chris Hadfield helped "unwrap" Canada's important contribution to the Station. It was carried into space in the payload compartment of the American Space Shuttle *Endeavour*. As usual, both Canadarms per-formed perfectly.

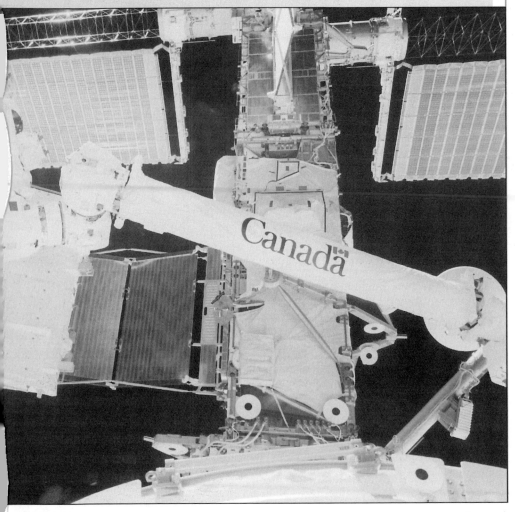

The Canadarms were designed by hundreds of top engineers and scientists from across the country. Using the arms, astronauts can carefully capture, move and place things in space. Large objects like the giant Hubble Space Telescope and the U.S. Lab Module for the Station can be placed within centimetres of the target site. This amazing accuracy is essential. Canadarm2 will act as the construction crane assembling the International Space Station until at least 2006. The Station could not be built without it.

The first Canadarm has performed perfectly on the more than 58 missions it has completed since 1981. It has placed new satellites into orbit and captured broken ones. Because of it, satellites can be repaired in space, saving satellite owners millions of dollars. The Canadarm also acted as a movable work platform for astronauts — a place to stand — in the first assembly mission of the Space Station, joining the U.S. Unity Node to the Russian-built Zarya Station.

The National Research Council hired Spar Robotics (now MD Robotics) to design, develop and build both Canadarms. Measuring 15.2 metres In length, the first Canadarm has two main booms attached to a motor-driven shoulder, with elbow and wrist joints, and a mechanical cage-like "hand" used to capture payloads. On Earth it weighs only 410 kilograms, yet it can move loads of up to 266 tonnes in space. Two special closed-circuit television cameras — the Space Vision System (SVS), designed by Art Hunter of Thunder Bay, Ontario — keep track of movements. Astronauts use hand controls, routed through programs in one of the space shuttle's computers, to move the arm, and they watch what they're doing through the SVS. More flexible than a human arm, the Canadarm can perform very complicated movements. It's made of steel, graphite-epoxy, bumpers of Kevlar (the same material as bulletproof vests), and electric cabling. A many-layered insulation blanket covers electric heaters to keep the arm's inside temperature the same, no matter how cold or hot conditions are in space. The first arm returns to Earth in the shuttle's docking bay after each mission.

Canadarm2 is a "bigger, smarter and more grown-up version of the shuttle's robotic arm," according to Chris Lorenz, manager of Mission Operations at the Canadian Space Agency. Weighing 1,800 kilograms, Canadarm2 is 17.6 metres long, with seven motorized

joints. Its bigger "muscle" allows it to help dock the entire Space Station. On the Mobile Base System (a sort of trolley), Canadarm2 can travel the whole length of the Space Station on rails. This and other complicated moves are possible because Canadarm2 has "hands" — Latching End Effectors — at both ends, and joints with a larger range of motion than either the first Canadarm or a human arm. Its greater flexibility allows it to flip end over end like an enormous acrobat or inchworm. In this way it can anchor itself at different base points — called Power Data Grapple Fixtures (PDGFs) — on the Station. Each PDGF can provide power, data and video.

Four colour cameras are mounted on Canadarm2. Its thicker booms are made of high-strength carbon-fibre thermoplastic. Permanently at home in space, the new arm can be repaired there, too. Unlike the original arm, it has a sense of touch via force sensors, and can automatically move to avoid collisions. Both arms can be disconnected from computer control and operated by hand controls.

On July 29, 2001, the Canadarm2 completed its first major mission, installing the Joint Airlock on the International Space Station. The first Canadarm helped by showing camera views and serving as a work platform for astronauts.

In 2003 the Canada Hand will be installed on Canadarm2. It's a robot with two mechanical arms of its own (the Canada Fingers),

video cameras, lights and specially adapted tools. With it, astronauts will be able to perform fine tasks from the safety of the Space Station. Dangerous space walks won't be necessary.

Canadarm2 is part of our "ticket to ride" on the International Space Station. Canadian scientists perform experiments both inside and outside the Station's labs, and Canadian astronauts sometimes spend months at a time on the Station.

As Chris Lorenz says, "Canada and Canadians are a big part of space exploration."

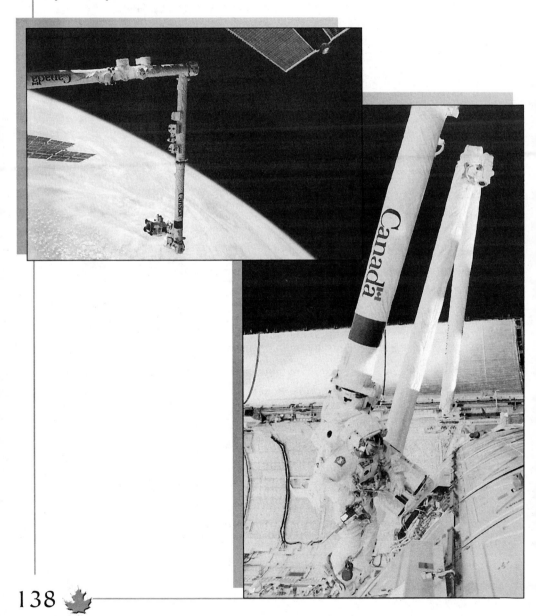

First Practical Electron Microscope

Ever seen the face of a virus — that all-but-invisible invader that can make you ill? Without the electron microscope, we would still be wondering about some of nature's most profound secrets, including viruses. The very first views into the very, very small were seen at the University of Toronto, in 1939. The first subject to be magnified was the edge of a razor blade. Under the best of existing microscopes that used light, the razor blade's edge looked crisp and even. But beneath the new 2-metre electron microscope, it became a series of jagged mountains and chasms. That was a day of great significance in the realms of science.

It took Dr. Eli Franklin Burton and his team at the Physics Department of the University of Toronto four years to build the first practical precision-working electron microscope. Ever since, tiny beings and objects have been photographed and studied in detail.

A crude model was first made by Dr. Ernst Ruska in Berlin in 1935. The machine was in its initial stages, not yet ready for scientists to reproduce and use. But the idea was brilliant. Burton visited Ruska and knew he had glimpsed the future. He was determined to be at the forefront of developing the amazing device.

As soon as he returned to the University of Toronto, Burton brought his gifted graduate students, James Hillier and Albert Prebus, on board to solve the engineering problems. Hillier and Prebus had to find ways of controlling a stream of electrons, directing them toward the target and capturing the image. Precise parts had to be individually machined and assembled. The team used electrical coils to direct the stream of electrons, and magnetic fields to focus the electron beam.

With the electron microscope, many branches of science have been revolutionized, especially biology and medical science. Centuries ago, in the late 1600s, the optic microscope invented by Dutch researcher Antonie van Leeuwenhoek enlarged objects using glass lenses under natural light. Light microscopes' viewing limit is about 10,000 units per centimetre. But up to 10 million units per centimetre can be viewed using the electron microscope.

A new wing at the University of Toronto was named the Burton Wing in recognition of Dr. Eli Franklin Burton's accomplishments as a scientist, teacher and inventor. James Hillier went on to design the first commercially manufactured electron microscope in North America for the Radio Corporation of America (RCA) in the United States. He continued to improve the electron microscope. The James Hillier Foundation in Brantford, Ontario, provides scholarships to science students in Canada.

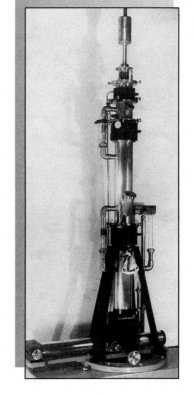

Electronic Sniffer
Is No Dog

How do you prevent dangerous materials from getting onto an airplane in the handbag, luggage or pocket of a passenger? Some of them might be small, or hidden in common objects, such as hair dryers or even the shoes a passenger is wearing. Not even X-ray machines can show everything, because anyone intent on getting something like a bomb onto a plane knows it will have to pass through an X-ray machine. Today there are many sophisticated ways of stopping people like terrorists from getting a dangerous object onto a plane — with more being developed all the time — but in the 1980s a device called the Explosives Vapour Detector (EVP) led the world in detecting dangerous and illegal substances at airports and embassies.

In the mid-1980s, Lorne Elias at the National Research Council (NRC) developed the EVP, a portable air analyzer to detect explosive material like gunpowder or plastic explosives, sensitive enough to register quantities as tiny as two parts per trillion of air. The handheld EVP unit took samples of air into glass cartridges with a pump. Then the suitcase-sized EVP testing unit checked them for signs of explosives. It took Elias eight years to create the convenient, sensitive device — a portable gas chromatograph. A silent display read ALARM if dangerous materials were detected, and rated the danger by number. Then dogs would be brought in to pinpoint the location of the problem.

Elias's original prototype EVPs were used to protect Pope John Paul II, Queen Elizabeth II and former United States President Ronald Reagan during their visits to Canada.

Lorne Elias always wanted to make the world a safer place. Born to Lebanese immigrants, he was deeply affected by the terrible human cost of bombs used in the 1948 Arab-Israeli war. He first designed machines to test for tiny amounts of insecticides in the air, as part of the NRC's fight against spruce budworm infestation in eastern Canadian forests. The machines could also monitor herbicides used on farms.

With the help of his student, André Lawrence, Elias then went on to create the Trace Narcotics Detector and the Ion Mobility Spectrometry (IMS) technique. Frank Karasek of the University of Waterloo had discovered the principles of IMS, which could detect both narcotics and explosives; Elias and his group made IMS work. Barringer Research of Toronto developed it further and the IMS became the new electronic sniffer. Even odour-free explosives didn't stop them — Elias and Pavel Neudorfl, an NRC colleague, found an ingredient to add to explosives so they would always have a smell. All plastic explosives manufacturers in the world agreed to include it in their products, in the interests of safety.

Today, new technologies employed by terrorists continually challenge security staff to find new forms of detection. But in the 1980s and early 1990s, airports and embassies around the world were safer because of the EVP and IMS, world leaders in vapour detection technology.

Making High-Speed Aerial Acrobatics Possible

Aircraft started out slow. They got faster and faster . . . until they hit a snag during World War II. Fighter planes could dive and turn at high speeds, performing as never before. The problem was that human beings couldn't keep up. High-speed turns or dives put so much centrifugal force on the pilot that he would lose his vision or black out. The cause was simple — the pilot's blood drained from his brain into his lower limbs. The result was a pilot out of control, and sometimes a downed plane. The Air Force asked medical researchers to solve fighter pilot blackouts. The Franks Flying Suit was the solution.

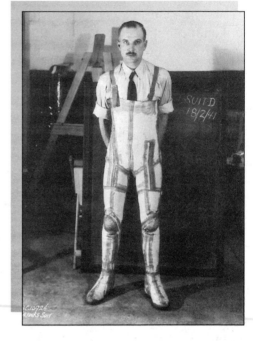

Wing Commander Wilbur Franks of Weston, Ontario, invented the world's first pressurized suit in 1940. Constructed by his team at the Banting and Best Medical Research Institute at the University of Toronto, it used water to protect the pilots.

Franks had first used water to protect test tubes in a centrifuge machine while doing cancer research. He imagined the pilot could be protected if surrounded by water — something like sitting in water in a full bathtub.

Other researchers laughed, but Franks and his team set about making the ridiculous possible. His suit was made of rubber, with pads full of water in the legs. In combination, the water and rubber kept pressure on the legs, and *that* kept pilots from blacking out. Franks himself wore the suit during flight tests, maintaining consciousness through forces almost eight times earth's normal gravity. He persuaded the Canadian government to build a human centrifuge to test it further. Introduced in 1942, his suit was a great success in World War II, and may have helped the Allies win the war in the air.

Franks's principles were later used to create space suits for astronauts. To supply the necessary pressure inside a space suit, though, air is used instead of water.

Son of Escaped Slaves Gives His Name to "The Best"

In the 1800s train travel had a big drawback. Steam engine parts would overheat and seize up, if used non-stop. The parts needed lubrication — oil to help the moving parts run smoothly — so trains had to make frequent stops to let the fireman drip oil onto every moving part, up and down the train and in the engine. Impatient passengers had to wait . . . and wait . . . and wait.

Enter Elijah McCoy. McCoy's parents had been slaves in the United States. They escaped to Canada in 1837 so their children could be educated — slaves were not allowed to read or write — and McCoy was born in Ontario, in freedom. Later his parents sent him to Scotland to become a trained engineer. But after his return to the U.S., the best job he could find in Ypsilanti, Michigan, as a Black man, was as a train fireman/oilman. He spent his days shovelling coal into the fire chamber of the steam engine, and running up and down the train, hand-lubricating moveable parts. McCoy saw the need for automatic lubricators, and worked in his shop at home for two years to create a self-regulating lubricating oil cup. It used steam pressure in cylinders to operate a valve and release the oil — a big improvement over any other lubricators at the time.

McCoy's system was ingenious. The cup that held the oil was built in as part of the steam cylinder. Oil could flow through a hollow rod attached to the base of the cup when the engine's steam pressure opened up the valve at the top of the rod. All this happened automatically as the steam engine's pistons moved up through the cylinder. So the engine regularly released oil from the cup to lubricate itself under normal running conditions. A year later McCoy changed his design so the oil would be released when the steam was spent. McCoy patented his oil cup in 1872. In later years he patented over fifty lubricating systems.

At first, white engineers were not interested in McCoy's invention. But, installed on trains under McCoy's supervision, the lubricator worked perfectly, and revolutionized railroad travel. The time needed for train travel was cut dramatically because no stops for lubrication were needed. Word spread. Soon other trains installed the lubricator, and within ten years it was used in mines and factories as well as on locomotives.

There were imitations of McCoy's device, but they didn't work nearly as well as his version, so people were soon asking for "the real McCoy." The new expression entered common speech, to mean "the best."

To find the time to work on his own inventions, Elijah McCoy moved with his wife to Detroit, Michigan, in 1882, and established his own company. His 87 other inventions include a folding ironing board, designs for tires and tire treads, a more durable rubber shoe heel, a lawn sprinkler and improved versions of his oil cup. Today, variations of McCoy's oil cup are still used in factories, mines, navy ships, construction machinery and space vehicles.

McCoy was a great engineering inventor. His advice to children was simple: "Stay in school. Be progressive. Work hard."

New Limbs for Kids

The Bloorview MacMillan Centre in Toronto, Ontario, is a world leader in designing electric limbs for children. Electric hands provide a strong grip, and look much like a normal hand.

Children with amputated arms or hands were once fitted with hooks at ages two or three. The child wore a harness with cables attached to it. The system was designed so shoulder movements could pull on the cables to operate the hooks, which could then grasp and use objects. But younger children didn't have strong enough shoulder motion to operate the hooks effectively. Now children as young as ten months can be fitted with electric hands and learn to operate them — a huge advantage, since the earlier children are fitted with artificial limbs, the more easily they adapt and become skillful.

An electric arm or hand can be controlled by signals from the child's existing or remaining muscles, or with switches. If it is controlled by muscle signals it is called myoelectric control. Development of electric limbs for children began in the 1960s at the Ontario Crippled Children's Centre in Toronto, now known as the Bloorview MacMillan Children's Centre, and also in Montreal and Fredericton. Tragically, numerous women in the late 1950s and early '60s had taken a drug called thalidomide during pregnancy, to relieve nausea, and many of their children were born missing limbs. (Before that, artificial limbs had been produced mostly for adults — including those injured in the two World Wars — not for children.)

Members of the Variety Club (Toronto) saw the need for a company to produce parts for artificial limbs for infants and children, so they established the Electrolimb Centre at Variety Village in 1970. The next year, researchers at Bloorview MacMillan collaborated with the Northern Electric Company to design the first electric hand small enough for a child. Swedish companies took that design and created the first myoelectric hands for children. At Bloorview MacMillan a series of smaller, lighter weight myoelectrically controlled hands were then designed — four sizes of hands for children were eventually produced — as well as wrist rotators for the hands, and two sizes of elbows for children.

This hardware is made and marketed the world over by Variety Ability Systems Incorporated (VASI), the only manufacturers of myoelectric elbows and wrist-rotators for children in the world. (Other companies produce hands for children.) In the past thirty years VASI has distributed more than 2,300 electric hands and 800 electric elbows, to improve the quality of life for thousands of children. Close collaboration between medical, engineering and manufacturing personnel is crucial. Each artificial limb is individually designed and made for the child in need.

Bloorview MacMillan fits about 70 children and adults each year, both from Canada and other countries. The Variety Club continues to financially support research and design of artificial limb components, and War Amputations of Canada helps pay for their production. Jenny Fredenburgh (below) holds the world's first programmable controller for prosthetic devices, developed at Toronto's Bloorview MacMillan Children's Centre.

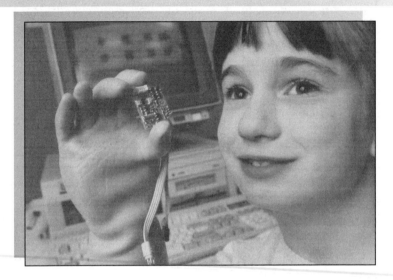

When Oil Is Spilled, Lick It Up

When a tanker ship carrying oil gets wrecked, the tragedy and loss have just begun. Crew members may lose their lives; the oil ship or company may lose hundreds of thousands — even millions — of dollars. But that's not the end of it. As the oil spreads, it can kill everything in its path — birds, seals, fish, every kind of sea or freshwater life.

Certain naturally occurring microbes can gradually break down the oil, converting it to safe substances. The sun can oxidize parts of thinly spread oil, and some will evaporate or disperse. But for large oil spills, nature's slow solution is not enough. When large quantities of oil are spilled into seawater or lake water, its poisonous effects continue for decades. The Slicklicker helps to clean up this environmental nightmare, and recover lost oil as well.

The Slicklicker is a simple machine with a huge impact. It has a metre-wide conveyer belt "tongue" made of terry cloth and canvas. Soaked in oil, the tongue attracts other oils and repels water. It picks up any kind of oil and carries it to a heavy wringer. Then the machine squeezes the oil into barrels, for later re-use, while the tongue returns to pick up more oil. The wringer removes most of the oil from the belt, but enough is left to attract more oil, and so on. One machine alone can lift 195,000 litres of oil in twenty-four hours, under good conditions. An inflatable plastic boom with a 1.5-metre skirt, mounted on a boat or barge, traps the oil close to the Slicklicker.

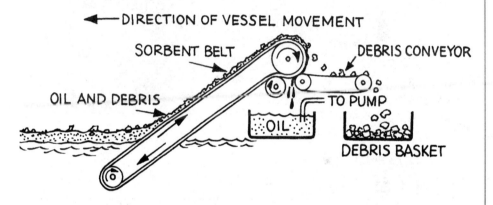

Richard Sewell, then a chemist with the Defence Research Board of the Department of National Defence, invented the Slicklicker in the late 1960s. It was soon needed desperately in Nova Scotia. On February 4, 1970, the Liberian tanker *Arrow* ran aground in Cheda-bucto Bay, spilling almost 10,000 tonnes of oil into gale-whipped sea waters. The oil floated to the surface of the water and spread out. Disaster was imminent, since a single barrel of crude oil can cover 30,000 square metres of seawater and nearby beach. Canada faced its worst marine pollution problem. If the oil could not be recovered, the Bay's sea and coast life would die.

Four Slicklickers were put to work as quickly as possible. In spite of the rough seas, the machines lifted almost a million litres of oil in the next ten weeks, and Chedabucto Bay was saved.

The safe, compact Slicklickers had proven themselves. Sewell and his brother manufactured them for Canada, England, Japan,

France, Israel and Borneo. Dec Doran, a member of the task force that cleaned up the massive 1989 *Exxon Valdez* spill in Alaska, says the Slicklicker is "one of the most important advances for oil spill recovery on water." Doran is now president of Oil Spill Control Services of Toronto, which uses fifteen versions of the Slicklicker in its work all over the world.

How often do oil spills happen? Too often. About 1,000 spills per year happened in Canada in the early 1990s. Luckily most of these were under 1 tonne.

* In the fight against oil spills, another Canadian innovation uses Side Looking Airborne Radar (SLAR). Dr. R. Goodman was working for Esso in Calgary when he developed the system. Ocean currents and winds can move oil spills long distances. Crews have to locate the oil accurately before clean-up can begin. They do this by tracking the spill from an aircraft using SLAR. Ultraviolet radiation reveals the presence of oil, and infrared radiation shows how thick the layer of oil is. The SLAR detects the calm in otherwise rough water caused by the presence of the oil.

* A leader in oil spills clean-up, Oil Spill Control Services also uses oil-eating bacteria, fungi and yeasts. Cleaning the environment is a constant battle.

Smart Money Discourages Counterfeiters

Money was invented thousands of years ago. Soon after, people began to counterfeit it. How can money be protected from clever fakery? Look at the top left corner of any Canadian banknote of $20 or higher, and you'll see a counterfeiter's nightmare — a thin iridescent optical film. This film cannot be reproduced without using a multi-million-dollar machine. It's just too expensive to fake.

The film was developed by George Dobrowolski and his team at Canada's National Research Council (NRC) in 1972. It took Dobrowolski's team ten years to perfect the technology. The film is as thin as the ink on the bill, so the banknotes are no thicker than they would be without the film. In 1988 the Bank of Canada began using thin optical film to protect $50 bills. Since then it has been applied to banknotes of $20, $100 and $1,000. Machinery and technical expertise aside, the thin-film devices are relatively inexpensive. And the patches are easy to spot, so Canadian money has become very hard to counterfeit.

Thin-film technology has been used on driver's licences in British Columbia, passports, personal identity cards and stock certificates. It also has applications in optical instruments, lasers, computers, solar cells, lens coatings, architectural glass, automobile glass and aerospace. Says Dobrowolski, "The NRC is one of the best environments in the world for a scientist to hope to work in."

A World Leader in Clean Energy for Cars

Ballard Power Systems is helping to make a pollution-free world possible, by replacing internal combustion engines with fuel cells. Ballard is the world leader in developing and supplying proton-exchange membrane (PEM) fuel cells — the fuel cells that might replace the car engine. (There are many other kinds of fuel cells, each with a different design.)

Internal combustion engines produce much of the energy in our modern world. They burn fossil fuels (for example, natural gas or gasoline) to produce electricity, to heat our homes and to move our planes, trains, buses, trucks and automobiles. But combustion engines also pollute the air, water and soil. Massive use of them has made smog in our cities and contributes to acid rain in our forests. Also, fossil fuels (so-called because they were created eons ago from decayed life forms) like oil and gas are being used up. When they are gone, we cannot replace them.

Here's where the fuel cell comes in. A fuel cell is much more like a battery than an engine. Instead of burning fuel, the fuel cell changes its fuel (hydrogen) and oxygen into electricity, water and heat. This makes it a nearly pollution-free source of energy. Fuel cells are not new. They've been firing scientists' imaginations for over a century. (A Welsh scientist built the first fuel cell in the late 1830s.)

With contributions from colleagues around the world, including scientists at Los Alamos National Laboratories in the United States, the people at Ballard learned how to create highly efficient fuel cells with large power outputs, for a size and cost that can be made affordable. How?

Ballard perfected the PEM fuel cell. In this cell, hydrogen gas flows in one end and oxygen is added at the other. An electrochemical reaction takes place inside the cell, made possible by a rubber-like membrane lightly coated with platinum (a unique feature of a PEM fuel cell; Ballard researchers learned how to keep the membranes active, with the hydrogen, water and oxygen flowing). The reaction produces electricity, which can power a car axle, light a bulb or do any other electrical work. Hot water is a by-product of the reaction. The water flows out of the power cell, and could be used to do something like filling a bathtub or heating a home. (So the fuel cell produces a second useful, non-polluting energy source!) Each fuel cell equals about a 0.7-volt battery; they can be stacked until the power level required is available.

An airport shuttle bus was the first vehicle to be powered by a fuel cell, in 1993. Fuel-cell-powered transit buses began running in Chicago and Vancouver in 1998. Fuel cells are being tested in prototypes of two vehicles, a Sprinter Van and a Chrysler Natrium. Hydrogen is supplied by a sodium borohydride storage system.

By the year 2004, low-pollution or pollution-free cars should be running on California roads. Methane is one possible source of the hydrogen that will be needed to power them. (Methane can be produced from manure, so it will not run out.) Ballard PEM generators for heating and lighting homes are slated for the Japanese market. Stay tuned for further developments on this cutting-edge technology.

The Inventor's Inventor

Wheelchairs were a great invention for people who could not walk. But what about people who couldn't use their arms either, like some veterans from World War II? For them, George J. Klein invented a motorized electric wheelchair with a "joy stick" hand control, so people with only partial use of their hands could control their own wheelchairs. This gave more independence to people with multiple disabilities. They no longer had to rely on someone to push their wheelchairs around.

Klein might have been the most productive inventor in Canada in the twentieth century. He discovered his interest in mechanical devices as a boy in his father's watch and jewellery store workshop in Hamilton, Ontario. After earning an undergraduate degree at the University of Toronto, he worked for the National Research Council. He stayed there for forty years, where he designed and built their first wind tunnels.

Without his work, skis might never have been fitted to aircraft. Klein was an internationally recognized expert on the mechanics of ice and snow. His research helped make winter air service to northern Canada possible. Aircraft with skis could land on snow-covered flat fields, improvised runways or frozen lakes.

Among Klein's many other inventions are these:

- He collaborated on the first successful microsurgical staple gun, used to suture blood vessels. This helped surgeons control bleeding and restore circulation more quickly.
- During World War II, Klein worked on creating stabilizing systems for anti-submarine mortars, fire-protection equipment, plus sighting devices and tracking systems for the U.S. military snowmobile the "Weasel," which was eventually used for scientific expeditions.
- He developed the Storable Tubular Extendible Member (STEM), a retractable antenna, in the early 1950s. A decade later the STEM was adapted for use in spacecraft. The antenna could be rolled into a small reel and unrolled in space. In this way, satellite antennas could be protected during blast-off, and unreeled later to lengths up to 45 metres. The applications of this one technology alone produced sales of over $10 million. The STEMs were vital parts of both the Gemini and Apollo Space programs. NASA used them for astronaut communications, and to collect and record sub-surface data transmitted from the moon, among other things. Without the success of STEMs, Spar Aerospace might not have become an independent Canadian company, and Canada might not have won the Canadarm project.
- Klein headed the team that designed Canada's first nuclear reactor.
- In 1976 he was called out of retirement to act as chief consultant on the gear design for the Canadarm project. He was then 72.

Klein died in 1992, at the age of 88. Colleagues remember him as a man of great enthusiasm, at work and in his leisure pursuits as a violinist, sailor and avid cross-country skier.

George Klein seated in the motorized wheelchair he designed

The User-Friendly Screwdriver

If you had X-ray vision and could look at all the fasteners that put together the room you're in — at home, at school or at the shopping mall — 85 percent of them would be Robertson screws. Peter Lymburner Robertson invented square-headed drivers and screws, and patented them in 1908. He was a tool specialist, and his clever system soon dominated the Canadian market.

There's a story about Robertson hurting his own hand when a slot-headed screwdriver slipped in his grasp. A tool expert, Robertson decided to invent a better screw and driver on the spot . . . and the rest is history, so the story goes.

Did it really happen like this? No one knows. But injuries like the one in the story have often occurred, since the slot-headed screw does not firmly anchor the screwdriver. Also, the slot in the screw can easily deform when pressure is applied to the driver, and the screw is ruined. By contrast, the Robertson screw fits so firmly to the driver that the screw can be mounted there, and then positioned — no slippage possible. It's a neat, rapid and easy solution.

Further refining his invention, Robertson created three sizes of

Robertson drivers and screws, their handles colour-coded green, red and black, from smallest to largest.

Builders, professional and amateur, took to the invention quickly. Not long after Robertson's invention, the Fisher Body Company (famous for building the Ford Model T) decided to use it in their production line.

Unlike the Canadian market, the United States has been slow to adopt the Robertson system. About 10 percent of screws sold there are Robertson, but use is now growing so fast that they could dominate the industry in fifteen years.

George H. Cluthe, owner of Waterloo, Ontario's, Cluthe Manufacturing Company, invented the interchangeable multi-headed screwdriver in 1965. All the common screwdriver heads are mounted on removable bits stored in the hollow handle of the screwdriver under a screw-off lid. In seconds the driver bit can be changed for differing jobs. Millions of the versatile tool are sold around the world today.

The Burpless Baby Bottle

If you've ever bottle-fed infants, you know they swallow air with their milk. Then they have to be burped, or the air causes pain in their stomachs. Burping is often a mixed success. Sometimes milk comes back up the baby's throat with the air.

Jean Saint-Germain, an inventor from Saint-Hyacinthe, Quebec, was living with his married brother in 1953 when he decided to change all that. He wanted a flexible container for the milk, instead of a rigid one. He first tried feeding his brother's baby from a bottle with a balloon liner, but the balloon material didn't easily collapse. Next Saint-Germain tried lining the milk bottle with a thinner plastic. As the baby drank the milk, the plastic liner collapsed. The baby swallowed much less air, and the need for burping was greatly reduced. If plastic bags of the right thickness were used, Saint-

Germain reasoned, a new sterile bottle liner could be used for each feeding. That would decrease the labour of sterilizing bottles as well.

Saint-Germain could not interest plastics manufacturers in his collapsible, disposable baby-bottle liner. A man from Baltimore bought his idea for $1,000 cash and sold it to Playtex Ltd. in the United States. Now over a billion of the liners are sold each year. Parents can prepare the feeding in advance and store or freeze the milk in the sterile liner. An estimated one quarter to one third of all infants in North America nurse from disposable plastic bags.

Saint-Germain also invented a brakeless motorcar and a musical wooden clock, as well as air-deflectors to streamline trucks and a motorized vest that could propel a cyclist, rower or skier. An avid parachutist and pilot, he designed his own ultra-light aircraft. Near Drummondville, Quebec, he built an Aerodium in which visitors could experience free fall. But none of these inventions was as successful as the baby-bottle liner idea that he had sold, and the inventor lived in poverty.

Acrylics Boost Safety

See-through unbreakable plastic makes it safer to ski, skin dive, ride a motorcycle and work in a woodshop. The reason is easy to see. Where protection for the eyes and good visibility are needed, nothing beats acrylics for goggles, face masks, helmets or safety glasses. Should an accident happen, the tough acrylic "glasses" won't shatter under a blow, as earlier glasses did.

Acrylics are used for many objects now — paperweights, art sculptures, food containers — the list goes on and on. Hospitals are safer with incubators for babies made of see-through plastic; airplane windshields made of acrylics withstand weather and even collisions with birds; deep-sea diving gear uses acrylics to combat crushing water pressure and give clear visibility. Dr. William Chalmers could never have foreseen all the uses of his invention when he created acrylics in 1931, as a graduate research student at McGill University in Montreal.

The transparent plastic used in thousands of everyday household and industrial items has a jaw-breaker of a name — polymerized methyl methacrylate. People tried to create methyl methacrylate polymers as early as 1877, but they never got a transparent plastic. Their early attempts were cloudy at best. Chalmers was the first to produce a clear, workable product. He sold his invention to Imperial Chemical Industries, which granted a license to DuPont to produce acrylics commercially. It is hard to imagine a world without them now — a contribution to safety and visibility in thousands of forms.

Garbage Bag Cleans Up

Three different Canadians claim that they invented the plastic garbage bag. The time was the late 1940s and '50s. Inventions often arise at the same time in different places because the need or technology or materials for the invention have become available. Who was really first? You decide.

After World War II, Harry Wasylyk of Winnipeg started making bags for fruits and vegetables out of the newest material in town — polyethylene. Wasylyk had been forced out of the canning business, and he needed a new product. He made the first bags in his kitchen and sold them to stores and plants around the city. He also sold plastic surgical gloves to the Winnipeg General Hospital. His hospital contacts told him how difficult it was to keep garbage cans free of contamination, so Wasylyk developed the plastic garbage bag to line the cans and keep the containers clean. From his kitchen the business moved to a plant.

At about the same time, Larry Hanson, manager at Union Carbide's plant in Lindsay, Ontario, was making garbage bags by hand for clean-up around the plant and to use at his cottage. Union Carbide bought Wasylyk's business, and decided the garbage bag was a great way to use up the almost 5 million kilograms of polyethylene resin sitting in the Montreal Union Carbide plant. Some towns and cities didn't want to switch to garbage bags, but Union Carbide persuaded Etobicoke, Ontario, to give them a try. Sales were slow at first, though hardware stores were willing to stock them. But when the Man from Glad promoted the bags in the 1960s (Union Carbide owned the Glad product line), larger stores carried them. Sales soared.

Also in the 1950s, Toronto's Frank Plomp, president of an envelope manufacturing company, got the idea for plastic garbage bags. He found a way to weld thin polyethylene film to form a tough bag with strong seams, and formed his own company to develop and sell the Garbag. In 1959 he began selling clear bags to hospitals and offices as liners for wastebaskets and garbage cans. Users of the Garbag saved on the costs of steam-cleaning the cans and baskets. In 1962 he made garbage bags green (to blend with lawns) and opaque (to hide the garbage from view). These bags were intended for home use. Trials in Waterloo, Ontario, showed that garbage bags were cleaner and quieter than garbage cans when the racket of cans being hefted, dumped and tossed back down was an unwelcome alarm clock in many towns. Plomp sold his bags to municipalities. They spread from small-town Ontario to Toronto and Montreal.

Who was the real inventor? Maybe all three!

Heads Up, Painters!

Have you ever tried to paint a whole wall — or even worse, a ceiling — with a paintbrush? That's almost a guaranteed paint-in-the-face exercise. Only professionals could get a good finish on walls or ceilings before Norman Breakey's invention. Breakey created the first paint roller in Toronto in 1940. Today, every home decorator would bless his name, if they knew it. With an inexpensive paint roller, even a beginner can tidily apply a smooth coat of paint to a ceiling or wall. Add a long handle to the roller, and the need for ladders almost vanishes.

Breakey's invention was elegantly simple, but brilliant. He had invented other things before, but he was convinced the paint roller would change the painting and home decorating industry in a big way. It would put home painting within reach of common men and women — why hire a painter when you can do the job yourself? Breakey was sure the paint roller would earn him a fortune.

He was right about the value of his invention, but he didn't get the fortune. Like too many other Canadian inventors, he struggled without success to get development funding. Soon after he began selling his paint roller, other variations hit the market too. In order to defend his patent, Breakey would have had to fight them all in court, but he didn't have the money to do it.

Breakey invented a few other useful items. He created a new piece of hardware to tap beer kegs, and an inventory system to help supermarket managers keep track of their stocks. But Breakey never made a fortune.

Zzzipping Along...

It's hard to imagine life without zippers. But the zipper was not easy to invent or perfect.

Whitcom Judson's Universal Fastener Company of Hoboken, New Jersey, wanted a better slide fastener because theirs often jammed, snapped and unfastened on its own. They turned to engineer Gideon Sundback, a Swedish-born Canadian immigrant. Sundback worked for four years in the early 1900s to produce the elegant and efficient interlocking-teeth Separable Fastener we now call the zipper. Good thing, too. The number of uses for the device is staggering.

Rubber galoshes made by B.F. Goodrich sported the first zippers. Just "zip 'er up or zip 'er down," Goodrich advertised. In the 1930s the clothing industry began to use zippers. Now, furniture and pillow coverings, backpacks, boat coverings (to keep out rough or rainy weather), plastic windows (such as those used for convertibles), luggage, pockets, pants, coats, boots and countless other articles sport zippers. They're used all the way from the remote Arctic to space shuttles.

Selected Bibliography

Black, Harry S. *Canadian Scientists and Inventors: Biographies of people who made a difference.* Markham: Pembroke Publishers Ltd., 1997.

Brown, J.J. *Ideas in Exile: A History of Canadian Invention.* Toronto: McClelland & Stewart, 1967.

Brown, J.J. *The Inventors: Great Ideas in Canadian Enterprise.* Toronto: McClelland & Stewart, 1967.

"Canadian Discoveries & Inventions." *Horizon Canada.* Brampton, ON: Centre for the Study of Teaching Canada, Oct. 1984–Jul. 1987.

Conacher, Duff. *More Canada Firsts: another collection of Canadian firsts & foremosts in the world.* Toronto: McClelland & Stewart, 2000.

Carpenter, Thomas. *Inventors: Profiles in Canadian Genius.* Camden East: Camden House Publications, 1990.

Guinness Book of Records. Enfield, England: Guinness Publishing, 1998.

Hancock, Pat. *Crazy Canadian Trivia.* Markham: Scholastic Canada Ltd., 2000.

Livesey, Robert. *Footprints in the Snow: The heroes and heroines of Canada.* Mississauga, ON: Little Brick Schoolhouse, 1978.

Mayer, Ron. *Inventing Canada: 100 Years of Invention.* Vancouver: Raincoast Books, 1997.

Mayer, Ron. *Scientific Canadian: Invention and Innovation from Canada's National Research Council.* Vancouver: Raincoast Books, 1999.

Nader, Ralph, Nadia Milleron & Duff Conacher. *Canada Firsts.* Toronto: McClelland & Stewart Inc., 1992.

Nostbakken, Janis & Jack Humphrey. *The Canadian Inventions Book: Innovations, Discoveries and Firsts.* Toronto: Greey de Pencier Publications, 1976.

Shell, Barry. *Great Canadian Scientists.* Victoria, B.C.: Polestar Book Publishers, 1997.

The Canadian Encyclopedia. Edmonton: Hurtig, 1988.

Verstraete, Larry. *Whose Bright Idea Was It? True Stories of Invention.* Markham: Scholastic Canada Ltd., 1997.

Index

Photo Credits

The publisher wishes to thank the following for providing photographs:

p. 18: (upper) CP/Mike Ridewood
p. 18: (lower) CP/Paul Chaisson
p. 25: *Bluenose*, By the wind, on lee side, full sail, 1922, courtesy of Knickle's
   Studio & Gallery, Lunenburg, N.S.
p. 28: Canadian Aviation Museum
p. 39: courtesy of Drumheller Regional Chamber of Development
   and Tourism
p. 40: © copyright TrizecHahn Tower Limited Partnership
pp. 43-44: courtesy of Gerry Fox
p. 49: courtesy of City of Greater Sudbury
p. 52: courtesy of Rosemary Withers
p. 56: courtesy of Dr. Tom Brown, Professor and Head of the Civil Engineering
   Department, University of Calgary Department of Engineering
p. 58: National Archives of Canada, PA-114787 and C67451
p. 61: National Archives of Canada, PA123481
p. 65: Myrna Maxwell, courtesy of Wendy Murphy, inventor of the WEEVAC
   stretchers
p. 72: © courtesy of Gail Harvey, photographer, and the Terry Fox Foundation
p. 74: Photo courtesy of the Rick Hansen Man in Motion Foundation
p. 75: Jean-Baptiste Benavent/Canadian Paralympic Committee (CPC)
p. 84: courtesy of Sharon Robinson
p. 93: Glenn Le Drew
p. 99 : © Canada Post Corporation, 1851, reproduced with permission
p. 101: Image courtesy of the Electronic Visualization Laboratory, University of
   Illinois at Chicago.
pp. 103, 104: courtesy of Ganong Bros. Limited
p. 108: National Archives of Canada, RD54
p. 122: National Archives of Canada, C17335
p. 127: courtesy of Rogers Communications, Inc.
pp. 135, 138: NASA: National Aeronautics and Space Administration,
   STS100-342-024, STS100-343-001, STS100-396-007
p. 140: University of Toronto Archives and Records Management Services
p. 142: National Archives of Canada, PA205374
p. 146: P. Power, The Toronto Star, courtesy of Bloorview MacMillan Children's
   Centre
p. 147: Oil spill diagram based on drawing from Dec Doran, Oil Spill Control
   Services
p. 148: courtesy of Dec Doran, Oil Spill Control Services
p. 150: courtesy of Ballard Power Systems
p. 153: National Research Council of Canada

The author wishes to thank the following for their kind assistance:

Lisa Cousins, Ph. D., sciences consultant and friend
Michael Bradford, research assistant and friend

Ian Anthony, Historian, Rogers Communications Inc.
Leanne Akehurst, Canadian Aviation Museum
Michel Bechar, Science North
Dr. Bertram Brockhouse, scientist
Dr. Randall Brooks, Curator, Physical Sciences & Space, Canada Science
   & Technology Museum
Chris Brown, Tourism Winnipeg
Gisele Charette, City of Greater Sudbury, Economic Development and Planning
   Services
Norine Charlie, Manager, Alert Bay Info Centre
Shira Cherns, Medical Services Associate, Novo Nordisk Canada, Inc.
Sherri Clegg, Communications Coordinator, West Edmonton Mall
Bob Davis, General Manager, Drumheller Regional Chamber of Development
   & Tourism
Dec Doran, President, Oil Spill Control Services
Renald Fortier, Curator, Aviation History, Canada Aviation Museum
Jesse Finkelstein, Publishing Assistant, Raincoast Books
Darrell Fox, National Director, The Terry Fox Foundation
Mike Gentry, NASA Public Affairs
Gerry Fox, photographer
Fiona Smith Hale, Canadian Aviation Museum
Sheila Hubbard and Louise Kinross, Bloorview MacMillan Children's Centre
Information Service, Greater Sudbury Public Library
Jan Innes, VP Communications, Rogers Communications Inc.
Christine Johnston, Macleans
Klay Kauback, Licensing and Distribution, Mainframe Entertainment Inc.
Kathleen Kemp, Professor, University of Toronto
Irene Knight, Manager, Public Relations, CN Tower
Rural Municipality of Armstrong
Chris Lorenz, Manager, Mission Operations, Canadian Space Agency
Glenn LeDrew, photographer and amateur astronomer
Mary Macchiusi, Pembroke Publishers
Sherry MacDougall, Communications Officer, Tourism, P.E.I.
Dr. Tak Mak, Professor, University of Toronto
Robin S. McGary, Harvard-Smithsonian Center for Astrophysics
Bill McGinty, Mines and Minerals Information, Ontario
Christoph McLellan, Drumheller Regional Chamber of Development & Tourism
Eric Mercer, Ph.D., scientist at large
Jane Mingay, Discovery Channel Canada
Karen Mortimer, Media Relations Officer, Canada Science & Technology Museum
Wendy Murphy, W. Murphy Enterprises Inc.
Beverly Orr, Center for Study of Responsive Law, Washington, D.C.
David Rudkin, Assistant Curator, Department of Paleobiology, Royal Ontario
   Museum